Women and Development:
Approaches and Perspectives

Women and Development:
Approaches and Perspectives

Edited By

Dr. Sudeshna Saha

KALPAZ

First Published, 2021

Published by

Kalpaz Publications
C-30, Satyawati Nagar,
Delhi – 110052
Ph.: 011-47034999, 9811692060
www.kalpazpublications.com
E-mail: kalpaz@hotmail.com

Printed at: Gyan Press, Delhi.

Cataloging in Publication Data—DK
Courtesy: D.K. Agencies (P) Ltd. <docinfo@dkagencies.com>

Women and development: Approaches and Perspectives / edited by Dr. Sudeshna Saha.
pages cm
Contributed articles.
Includes index.
ISBN 9789353242862 (HB)

1. Women in development—India. 2. Women—Health and hygiene—India. I. Saha, Sudeshna, editor.

LCC HQ1240.5.I4W66 2020 | DDC 305.420954 23

Contents

Preface

This book is a compilation of papers authored by academicians, scholars, practitioners who are themselves witness to the growing challenges of women in their day-to-day lives. Women comprise of half the world's population and it is she who bears and gives birth to the male folk, much to become victims in their hands. Women sacrifice their whole lives doing non- economic chores which apparently seem unworthy and invisible. She struggles throughout her life to balance all the odds of her family and society. Still she feels unsafe, weak, secondary and sometimes a burden for her household. She is supposed to be fit only for bearing, rearing and caring children. She silently bears all the torments of life, be it sexual violence, domestic violence, eve teasing, acid attacks, emotional abuse, economic dependency and related torture. Patriarchy is reinforced by women themselves. The voice of women are kept unheard, their struggles for justice is hushed up before it reaches the authorities, their rights are suppressed, justice denied to her. But if we deny and defy their rights and privileges then we do social injustice. A woman weeps which means her family weeps, society weeps and so does the entire nation. Women do possess the rights to education, better health, family planning, security for livelihood. In today's world, women walk shoulder to shoulder with men and excel in every sphere of human lives. The book is a small tribute to celebrate the omnipresence of women in each areas of life. It therefore focuses on women's health status, educational scenario, food habits, life style, livelihood, women's struggle in informal sector and their need for digitalization. The book unfurls the intricate journey of women throughout her life and how their struggles bear fruits and they emerge winners and how history bears testimony of how they compassionately withstand their struggles of life and come-out successfully.

The book is dedicated to my dearest husband, who burnt the midnight lamp to do the corrections, referencing and plagiarism check without his major support the book editing would not have been possible, my sincere dedication to my parents, brother and all my fellow authors, friends and well wishers, who supported me in editing my first book.

Foreword

I feel privileged to write the foreword for the book titled "Women and Development". This edited volume is an outcome of various research papers on issues pertaining to women, with focus on health, nutrition, education, sustainable livelihood, condition in unorganized sector and impact of digitalization. The book further reflects on crosscutting issues of gender equality and position of women within the current socio-economic context. According to Nobel Laureate Amartya Sen, development is a gradual process of expanding freedom equally for all people (https://developmenteducation.ie/feature/women-development/). But the role of women is often seen only in relation to domestic space. While the role of women within the household context is critical, it is the most important to understand women's contribution to and in connection with the larger development process. The Sustainable Development Goal 5 of the United Nations recognizes achieving gender equality and empowering all girls as a key milestone for all countries. While countries have been focusing on gender equality and inclusivity in all policies and programmes, research evidence has shown the critical equity gaps still exist in women's workforce participation, health, education, employment and other such relevant areas. Gender equality is thus at the core of realizing all the sustainable development goals. Gender issues have remained invisible in several cases, as these are only being identified in situations where there is an evident crisis. Therefore, there is an ardent requirement of gender mainstreaming across all sectors and any form of resistance to gender equality must be eliminated. Gender mainstreaming and intersectionality as key processes have been largely recognized as impactful tools and methods by national, sub-national and international organizations in their advocacy and programmatic support to Government and other community based programmes. I hope, this book will provide an opportunity for innovative discussion to visualize woman's role and position in the development context from multi-pronged perspective. It may facilitate the reader to understand the position of gender in its powerrelations. I further, wish the editor and all authors of this book a great success in their advocacy for gender equality.

Mr. Sandipan Paul
Education Specialist, UNICEF Pacific

List of Contributors

1. Dr. Amrita Dey, Assistant Professor, Department of Sociology, Government General Degree College, Lalgarh, Jhargram, West Bengal. Address – AD-187, Sector 1, Salt Lake City, Kolkata-700064.
2. Dr. Tanushree Paul, Assistant Professor, Department of Women's Studies, Visva-Bharati, Santiniketan. Address- UF 04, Block -07 Appayan Apartment, Sukantapally, Santiniketan -731235.
3. Dr. Nabaruna Mazumdar, Assistant Professor, Department of Sociology, Gurudas College, Kolkata. Address- P133A, Lake Terrace, 3rd Floor, Kolkata -700029.
4. Dr. Ruchiraj Uphadyay, Assistant Professor, Department of Sociology, Bhaktakavi Narsinh Mehta University, Junagadh.
5. Ms. Meeraba Jadeja, Research Scholar, Department of English, Bhakta Kavi Narsinh Mehta University, Junagadh, Gujarat, Pin Code- 362001.
6. Dr. Kannappa V. Shetty, Psychosocial Consultant, Abhaya Hospital, Bangalore.
7. Mrs. Prerna Srivastava, MPhil Psychology Intern. Address-Psycho Social Consultant, Abhaya Hospital, Hosur Road, 7th Cross, Wilson Garden, Bangalore-560027.
8. Dr. Sudeshna Saha, Assistant Professor, Department of Social Work, Visva-Bharati, Santiniketan. Address- SF-05, Block 04, Appayan Apartment, Sukantapally, Santiniketan -731235.
9. Dr. Neelmani Jaysawal, Assistant Professor, Department of Social Work, Visva-Bharati, Santiniketan.
10. Dr. Swati Chakrabarty, Faculty, Human Rights, Schoolguru Eduserve Pvt. Ltd. India. Vice President- South East Asia, Eurasian Doctoral Summer Academy (EDSA) and International Fellow, KAICIID, Vienna. Address-18/1, Bhattarcharya Para Lane, P.O– Satragachi, Howrah - 711104, West Bengal.
11. Mr. Ashish Kumar Singh, Doctoral Candidate of Political Science, National Research University-Higher School of Economic, Moscow. Address-Room Number- 930, Dubki Dormitory, Denisa Davydova, VNIISSOK, Odintsovo, Moscow Region, Russian Federation, Pin- 143072.

1

Introduction

— ***Dr. Sudeshna Saha***

Development is a process that signifies a state of evolution, maturity, completeness, improvement and positive changes transiting to a desirable level of quality of life. Women have the subordinate status and position in the gender relationship and therefore they experience social structural inequalities and injustice in their everyday lives. This is the reason that women are given special treatment in the development process and women's development becomes the prime concern in policies and programs. It helps the women to strengthen their capacities and overcome the barriers experienced by them because of their sex. It recognizes both the productive contributions of women to the society (https://www. ijser.in/archives/.pdf). Indian scholar, economist and philosopher Amartya Sen sees development as a gradual process of expanding freedom equally for all people (https://developmenteducation.ie/feature/women-development/). Gender equality, from this perspective, is a core objective of development in itself implying that 'just as development means less income poverty or better access to justice, it should also mean fewer gaps in well-being between males and females (World Development Report, 2012). Yet, today's development realities beg the question as to whether we are achieving this objective sufficiently and in a reasonable timeframe. Although there has been considerable and important progress in terms of women's well-being (in rights, education, health and access to jobs etc), what of their 'ill-being'? It is still the case that no country treats women the same as its men (https://developmenteducation. ie/feature/women-development/).Although things have improved a lot in several domain, but gender-based equality is still a distant dream. Women still face a lot of social exclusion based on caste, creed, disability, location, ethnicity and sexual orientation. The role of women in developing countries, as explored throughout this module, has been recognized as the single most important factor when it comes to bringing about and sustaining long term social change. Women are farmers and food providers (contributing to agricultural output, general environmental maintenance and food security); they are business people and traders (40 percent of the world's labour force are women, not including informal work in the home, on the land, in the market place etc); they are heads of households (most of whom are likely to also have a full time job, as well as caring for children, elderly or sick relatives); they are mothers, care givers and support workers (more often than not, in developing countries, this is voluntary); and they are community leaders, activists and role models. Development affects men and women differently, often with a more negative impact on women. This can undermine women's role, status and position within society and therefore perpetuates their inequality. Women's equality is vital to sustainable development and the realization of human rights for all. Equality for women is vital economically, politically, socially, culturally and environmentally it is also crucially a matter of basic human rights (https://developmenteducation.ie/feature/ women-development/). Although the Beijing World Conference had emphasized the importance of women's participation in all areas of decision making and particularly in politics, the political dimension of main streaming was not strongly emphasized until after the Beijing conference. Women had begun to realize that, in most developing countries, gender mainstreaming initiatives mainly involved men because the mainstream was male dominated.

Women have a stronger personal interest in the advancement of women and, with the support of an active and vocal women's constituency, can strengthen overall political commitment to gender equality. Mainstreaming women or women in politics strategies focus on putting women's issues and priorities on the mainstream agenda through the direct political participation of women leaders supported, and held to account, by strong and active women's constituencies. Women-specific projects have been designed to achieve particular objectives, for example, the education of girls and women, women's autonomy, the gains of organizing, access to income, articulateness, support to widows, etc (https://crawford.anu.edu.au/ rmap/devnet/devnet/db-64.pdf). The practice of development has shown that women focused, as well as gender-focused approaches may redistribute power in social relations, or may not. Women's needs do not exist in isolation, but form part of an interconnected system of social and power relationships, including gender relations (https://crawford.anu. edu.au/rmap/ devnet/devnet/db-64.pdf).Gender mainstreaming seeks to integrate men and women's experiences and needs into development at all levels. This combined with specific actions for women's empowerment, is viewed as an essential means for the promotion of gender equality. Gender mainstreaming seeks to include both women's and men's concerns and experiences in overseas development projects and in the design, implementation, monitoring and evaluation of all legislation, policy and programs across government departments, so that women and men benefit equally (https://crawford.anu.edu.au/rmap/devnet/devnet/db-64. pdf). Gender issues have become invisible or marginalized, only being picked up in situations where there is a crisis or problem. Achieving gender equality outcomes requires leadership, staff capacity and internal and external champions (https://crawford.anu. edu.au/rmap/devnet/devnet/db-64.pdf). Gender mainstreaming is a synthesizing concept that addresses the wellbeing of women and men. It is a strategy that is central to the interests of the whole community (https://crawford.anu.edu.au/rmap/devnet/devnet/db-64.pdf). Gender mainstreaming was adopted by the UN as the key methodology for achieving gender equality following the UN Fourth World Conference on Women in Beijing, 1995 (https:// crawford.anu.edu.au/rmap/devnet/devnet/db-64.pdf). Gender mainstreaming is a political process that alters the balance of power; it is inherently 'complex and resistance will come in many forms. Jahan (1995:13) categorizes mainstreaming approaches as 'integrationist' and 'agenda-setting' or 'transformative'. The integrationist approach involves broadening the dominant paradigm to fit women 'in' without directly challenging power structures. Gender mainstreaming and intersectionality have become buzz words among women and men who work primarily as bureaucrats in the large national and international organizations that have become so powerful in the last decade or so (https:// crawford.anu.edu.au/rmap/devnet/devnet/db-64.pdf). Focusing only on women, in relation to such issues as economic participation, credit, or sexual and reproductive health for example, can leave women with yet more work to do and thus intensify gender inequalities. By the mid-1980s, UNIFEM and women's groups were beginning to recognize the need for a new approach that focused more explicitly on working with mainstream institutions and the comparison between the lives and experiences of women and men. The book will focus on various issues ranging from health status of women in India, impact of digitalization on women, common psychological problems among Indian women, Food-gender stereotype, education in tribal women, women workers in unorganized sector, de-gendering women: A human rights-based approach and addressing malnutrition among women and children in the developed and developing States. This book will highlight overall women-centered development paradigm.

References

- Women and Development, (excerpted from https://developmenteducation.ie/feature/womendevelopment/ on 13-06-2020).
- Development Bulletin, (excerpted from https://crawford.anu.edu.au/rmap/devnet/devnet/db-64.pdf on 23-05-2019).
- World Development Report, 2012: Gender Equality and Development, (excerpted from https://openknowledge.worldbank.org/handle/10986/4391 on 18-04-2020).

2

Health Status of Women in India: A Critical Analysis

— Dr. Amrita Dey

Introduction

In developing countries, health status of the marginal sections always remains at the threshold. In case of women, this marginality gets multiplied due to the fact that they always remain the second citizen. This chapter aims to explore and analyze the health status of women in India. Simple as it sounds, the general commonsensical notion stands true; the health conditions of women are still deplorable and in spite of developmental policies and policy implementation the improved statistical data remains inconclusive of the true status of women. In the initial section of the chapter, the objective is to provide some idea of the status of healthcare for women in India, as found in surveys, studies and reports. The important point here is that the injustice, patriarchy, gender bias and profit-motive identified in healthcare system are historically rooted in the history, tradition and culture of Indian Society. It is evident mostly in the ever increasing crime and violence against women which indirectly but enormously affect women's health status. A summary of the development and policies in the following section reaffirms the fight against injustice through recognition of Right to Health and gender inclusive development processes. But the paradox continues in the way that the family planning program in India based on bio-medical model put the dignity, respect and trust of women in India at stake. An exploration of ground realities in the next section heightens the paradox inherent in the system. It becomes clear that a new women-centric approach to health and healthcare is necessary. Theoretical insights discussed in the last section strengthens the argument that treating women's health as a medicalized reality will only make women more vulnerable as she will lose control, capacity to choose and to decide; her agency will remain completely ignored.

The discussion below is a time-constrained attempt to understand the inherent contradictions of the system; it can be read as a preliminary (with limitations) critical exploration of the present issue.

Health Status of Women in India: Past and Present Scenario

A study by Ramalingaswami (1987) on disadvantaged sections of women; tribal and rural married mothers at the age group of 15 to 45 years and their access to healthcare in a backward district of Visakhapatnam showed a grim picture. It is examined whether these mothers are aware of auxiliary nurse and midwives services, of tetanus toxoid injection, do they have knowledge of family planning, about Tuberculosis, leprosy and malaria. It is found that tribal women almost have no access to these services though they are aware of them. Compared to tribal women, rural women were better off. Basically there was marked differences as to how government programs reach different sections of women. Maternal and Child Health is almost found to be nonexistent in tribal areas. Ironically, family planning program with targets, pressure and propaganda did reach the tribal people. According to World Bank (1996) it is reported that health improvement among women in India lags, particularly among North Indians. A large number of girls under age of five dies and excess female mortality persist up to the age of thirty years. General morbidity level among Indian women is high. There is high prevalence of reproductive tract infections and Human Deficiency Virus-Acquired immunodeficiency syndrome (HIV-AIDS). High nutritional deficiency is also reported such as iron deficiency. It is actually a vicious cycle. A nutritionally deficient mother delivers low birth weight babies and thus the female child is disadvantaged from the very beginning due to undernourishment. Maternal mortality is reported as 15 percent of all deaths. Cause of deaths ranged from sepsis1, hemorrhage, lack of care, inadequate detection and illegal abortion. Maternal mortality is linked to maternal morbidity due to poor nutrition and anemia. World Bank report specifically mentions the Hindi belt consisting of Uttar Pradesh, Bihar, Madhya Pradesh, and Rajasthan. The report discusses about poverty and low level of education and awareness level as causes of poor health status of women. Women from lower socioeconomic status show inability in decision making and less control over resource allocation such as health care and food. Early marriage cause limited education among women and they are less likely to be aware of preventive and curative health care. Pregnancy is not considered as a condition requiring medical attention, even in the event of complications. In rural areas women mostly give birth at home. Purity pollution concepts associated with childbirth leads to unsanitary deliveries, leading to sepsis and neonatal tetanus in absence of proper immunization[2]. Also in number of essential areas to women's health, traditional beliefs come in conflict with modern medicines. For examples, they show superstitious inhibitions against oral tablets of folic acid or have detrimental disbelief of IUD3 and abortion. According to World Health Organization (WHO) statistics, in 2004, India had a tenfold greater mortality rate compared to China (Ma and Sood, 2008, p. 13). The average life expectancy of Indian women was 63 years whereas for women in China it was 74 years. Velkoff and Adlakha (1998) root the causes of high mortality rate among women in their social status and preference of male child within patriarchy. Female health problems are accentuated by high level of fertility (up to five children per women) which in turn is caused by high infant mortality rate and preference of a son. Numerous pregnancy and closely spaced birth negatively affects pregnancy outcomes such as premature births, low birth weight babies and health risk of mothers. There is also the negative impact of unwanted pregnancies and unsafe abortion. In 1993 high maternal mortality rate was reported (453 deaths per 100,000 births) (Velkoff and Adlakha, 1998, p. 3). LowestMaternal Mortality Ratio (MMR4) was in Kerala (87) whereas Madhya Pradesh and Orissa reported ratio over 700. The difference was due to difference in socio-economic status of women and different health care services provide by the states. According to National Family Health Survey (NFHS) conducted in 1992-1993, four years preceding the survey, 37 percent of all pregnant women in India received no pre-natal care, especially the women in rural areas(Velkoff and Adlakha, 1998, p. 4). Also three fourth of all births were taking place at homes, two-thirds were not attended by trained medical personnel (Velkoff and Adlakha, 1998, p. 4). 50 percent to 90 percent of pregnant women suffered from anemia. Severe anemia accounted for 20 percent of maternal deaths in India as it increases the chance of hemorrhage during labour. Nutritional deficiency and health concerns are also high in case of women and children in India. Their survival is threatened which is compounded by heavy work demands, poverty, childbearing, rearing and so on. Prevalence of HIV-AIDS is also found to be high among pregnant women in 1995; in the state of Tamil Nadu the percentage of infected pregnant women increased from 0.2 percent in 1989 to 0.8 percent in 1991 (Velkoff and Adlakha, 1998, p. 8). Allendorf (2013) made a study (from 1992 to 2006) based on NFHS (2005-2006), to explore if women's health especially that of young married women is benefitted if women transit from extended patrilocal families to nuclear family. The result is not affirmative; changes in the living arrangements of young women in nuclear family do not bear any advantages towards their health. The study used eight measures of health; these measures were indicators of maternal health and care, antenatal care, delivery assistance, indicators of women's diet and nutrition, anemia, dairy consumption, meat consumption, indicators of domestic violence, risking injury and poor self-report on health. Mediating variables included economic status and decision- making power. It is found that in the 14 years period between 1992 and 2006, the percentage of women living in nuclear family arrangements have increased by eight percent. It is also found that extended family has more benefits for young women's health. Here women are less likely to be anemic, they receive better antenatal care and delivery assistance and they experience less physical violence. On the other hand, women in nuclear family have advantage of higher meat consumption. However physical and sexual violence is reported within both the family structures. In-laws are more likely to suppress violence. The higher economic status of extended family also has health benefits for women. However, the difference in family structure in India, is argued to be and ambiguous; family members can share resources and decision-making across household structures especially if they live nearby. Overtime, education of women, strengthening of marital bonds over consanguineal bonds5 and not transit to nuclear family have improved the health status of young daughter in laws. Recent study on women's health status in India criticizes the fact that even after criticism of the bio-medical model, the focus still remain more on sexual and reproductive health (SRH) and not on non-communicable diseases (NCDs) such as diabetes and hypertension. Despite higher life expectancy women have higher burden of disability due to NCDs, back pain, depressive disorder and respiratory diseases as reported in 2016 by the policy report of The George Institute (https://www.georgeinstitute.org/sites/default/files/framing-womenshealth- issues-in-21st-century-india.pdf). The report specifies that all the stakeholders need to advocate and promote women's right to health through the integrated life-course. Gender equality/equity, empowerment, elimination of discrimination are critical to strengthen and protect women's health. The report also asks to engage with high risk behaviour among women such as smoking through communication and awareness building. Given that housewife constitute largest demographic group among suicide deaths in India (20 percent of all deaths in last 25 years), mental health disorders among women also need to be addressed. Violence against women (VAW) affects women's health status to a great extent. In 2013, WHO declared that VAW is a health problem of epidemic proportion (Edmunds and Gupta, 2016). WHO reported that globally one among three women suffer from intimate partner violence (IPV) and non-partner violence. These global finding are also corroborated in India. According to NFHS and National Crime Records Bureau (NCRB) the incidents of VAW is increasing since 2009 and IPV is 40 times higher than violence by non-partner violence. The national average of rape incidents in 2013 is 5.7 per 100,000 women. According to NCRB report in 2017, crime against women is registered as cruelty by husband and his relative (33.2 percent), assaults on modesty (27.3 percent), kidnapping and abduction (21 percent) and rape (10.3 percent) (NCRB, 2017). According to NFHS-4 (2015-2016), there is a decline in fertility rate from 2.7 in 2005-06 to 2.2 children per women. The median age of first birth is 21 years. Eight percent of women at the age group of 15-19 years (teenage) begin childbearing, which is high in rural areas. Just fewer than 50 percent opt for family planning and use contraceptive. Only 36 percent have gone for female sterilization. Almost one in five women suffers from complications due to abortion. The proportion of women receiving antenatal care has risen from 77 percent to 84 percent in 2015-16. About 89 percent women are protected against neonatal tetanus. According to NFHS, MMR has improved. In 1992-93, MMR was 437; in 2011-13 it declined to 167. In 2014-15, MMR was 130 per 100,000 live births[6].

Development and Policy Implementation: Right to Health and Inclusion on Gender

The right to health and life of dignity was first internationally recognized the constitution of World Health Organization in 1946. It is declared by WHO that having the higher attainable level of physical and mental health is one of the fundamental right of human being irrespective of race, religion, political belief and economic and social conditions. It is also declared that a state of complete physical, mental and social wellbeing is not merely the absence of any disease. According to the Fact Sheet No. 31 published by OHCHR7 and WHO (2008) Article 25 of The Universal Declaration of Human Rights health is a part of the rights required in order to maintain adequate standard of living. International treaties on human rights have since then also recognized the right to medical care. These treaties are relevant to every country. Each and every country has ratified at least one international human right treaty to recognize the right to health and have promised to be committed to these rights through domestic legislations and treaties. The right to health is an inclusive right and goes beyond the right to healthcare to include other socio-economic cultural factors that are essential to sustain health. These are access to safe drinking water and food, proper sanitation, healthy working environment, proper information and education related to health and gender equality. Right to health also involves fight to freedom, freedom from any inhuman treatment or non-consensual medical intervention such as forced sterilization. The right to health consists of certain entitlements; few of which are the rights to prevention, treatment and control of diseases, access to essential medicines, maternal, child and reproductive health. There should not be any discrimination in providing health services. All health services must be accessible, acceptable, and available and of good quality that is being scientifically approved.

The right to health have particular significance to specific groups such as women, children, disabled people that is people who are at some form of disadvantage conditions due to various socio-economic factors. Women suffer from the same health conditions as men but they experience these differently due to their economic dependence, gender bias, less power to have control over their sexual and reproductive lives and lack of decision-making capacities. All these factors negatively impact their health. Discrimination becomes manifold for women with disability, female refugees, women in slum and rural areas, and women living with HIV/AIDS. The important treaties specifically addressing women health are: (i) Convention on the Elimination of All Forms of Discriminations against Women, Art 12, according to which all State Parties will take measures to eliminate all discrimination against women and ensure women's access to health care and family planning on the basis of their equality to men; it would ensure services and nutrition to women in relation to pregnancy, confinement and post –natal period; (ii) International Covenant on Economic, Social and Cultural rights, Art. 10 (2), according to which it is necessary to ensure special protection to mothers for a reasonable period during and after childbirth, working mothers should be accorded paid leave and leave with social security benefits. Women should also have control and decision making power over their sexual and reproductive health. (iii) The Program of Action of International Conference on Population and Development (ICPD) 1994 and The Beijing Platform of Actions (Fourth World Conference on Women 1995) highlighted the right of both men and women to have access to safe, effective, affordable and available method of family planning. (iv) Violence against women also cause widespread damage to their physical and mental health, as such the Committee on the Elimination of Discrimination against women requires states to enact and enforce laws to protect women against violence, investigate such violence, prosecute perpetrators and the survivors of such violence are ensured the right to adequate reparation and rehabilitation to recover their physical and mental health. The UN Women works to prevent violence against women, the health consequences of which can be borne by generations. Survivors of sexual assaults need a series of sexual and reproduction health services. UN Women advocates states and support non-governmental partners to provide better coordinated health services to survivor of violence. They also work to end practices that are harmful for mother and child such child marriage, female genital cutting, and dietary restrictions. They also work to empower women living with HIV/AIDS. Sustainable Development Goal (SDGs) adopted by United Nation Member States in 2015 is an universal call to action to end poverty; protect the planet and ensure that all people enjoy peace and prosperity by end of 2030. The pledge is to 'Leave No One Behind' and countries have ensured fast track development for those who are left furthest behind. SDGs are integrated together to bring an end to poverty, hunger, AIDS and discrimination against women. SDG 3 specifically calls for action to ensure healthy lives and promote well being for all at all ages. It calls to reduce the global MMR to less 70 per 100,000 live births by 2030; to ensure universal access to sexual and reproductive health care services including family planning, information and education and the integration of reproductive health into national strategies and programs.

India was first among the developing countries to introduce family planning program, but from 1960s onwards in spite of all efforts population grew by two percent annually. MMR in India in 1990 following NFHS 1 (1992-1993) was highest in the world (550 deaths per 100,000 live births) (Visaria, Jejeebhoy and Merrick, 1999,p.S44). There were certain changes made in government policies in context of women's health. Method of specific family planning program was introduced in mid-1960s with primary focus on sterilization. In 1997, the program was reoriented to shift the overall approach in order to broadly address the limitations. The focus shifted to reproductive health, client choice, service quality, gender issues, and marginal groups such as menopausal women. It was noted that family planning program suffered due to centralized planning, target setting and these program allowed limited innovations. In mid-1970s government again went on to follow vigorous sterilization so much as to outrage women's organization due to violation of human rights. Later, it concluded in consensus by policy makers that ethical consideration, proper procedure, high quality care cannot be compromised in a zealous pursuit of demographic goals. The ICPD 1994 at Cairo acted as a milestone. World

Conference on Women at Beijing 1995 also added pressure from global community and this bought about a change in focus in Indian Family Planning Program. The significant changes that took place in government policies were; (i) active partnership with network of NGOs; (ii) in 1996 government took the bold step of making family planning program target free which in turn weakened the program at local levels and (iii) in 1997 government launched Reproductive and Child Health (RCH) program. The RCH programs removed all targets, provided incentives payments to followers and acceptors of family planning method, took help of voluntary and private organization, created forums for policy dialogues, information, education and communication and supervised periodic reviews. According to Visaria et al (1999) the challenge for government at that time was to strengthen client-centred approach in health system. Women themselves are meant to choose the method of contraception based on what she desire and not the service provider. Women are to be fully informed while taking decision about contraception, about the methods, about after care and about possible complications. It was emphasized that the service providers will consider the constraints women face such as vulnerability, lack of autonomy, unequal social status, and limited access to economic resources while catering for them. Health workers also need to be adequately trained and properly motivated. The evaluating and monitoring system may act as a model but it has to be adopted for each state and region so that each region has the flexibility to decide on its priorities. The awareness and education program must go beyond the aim of delivering information and awareness about contraception and small family; it need to assess local narratives, perspectives and believes regarding reproductive health because the messages communicated by government and nongovernmental organizations need to comply with the culture, language and needs of the community.

National Health Policy (NHP) (2017) follows the same guideline as NHP of 1983 and 2002. According to this particular document, maternal and child mortality have drastically declined. NHP (2017) recognizes the importance of SDGs. It also seeks to attain preventive and promotive healthcare, universal access to healthcare and lowering the cost of quality healthcare. It emphasizes on equity in healthcare, lessening all disparities and specifically gender disparity; healthcare is to be gender sensitive and patientcentered. Its objective is to assure the availability of free primary healthcare services associated with all aspects of reproductive, maternal, child and adolescent health. It seeks to strengthen the trust of common people on public healthcare system. The policy thrust is in attaining preventive and promotive health by aligning with the international call for 'Health in All' approach alongside the call for 'Health for All' (p. 3). One of the priority areas is action against gender violence. Occupational health is also being focused. Accredited Social health Activist (ASHA) along with other health workers as a part of the community and local self government and Village Health Sanitation and Nutrition Committee (VHSNC) is made responsible for primary preventive care and community and homebased palliative care. Maternal and child survival is ensured through program such as RMNCH+ A8. This policy aspires to elicit developmental action of all sectors to support maternal health and survival. It recommends strengthening of general health system to support, prevent, and manage maternal complications, to ensure care and emergency services for maternal health. It seeks to address all factors in a comprehensive manner in context of maternal health. Special attention is given to the addressing of malnutrition and micronutrients deficiency by creating awareness, through providing fortified food and food supplements. The Department of Women and Child Development is associated in this context to ensure that the deficiencies are addressed as early as possible. NHP (2017) also focuses on mental health and wants to increase the number mental of mental health specialist within public healthcare system, create network of community members for psycho-social support. Population stabilization is also important for all around development. However it wants to move away from camp-based services in order to protect the dignity, quality of life and safety of women. It aims to increase male sterilization from the current five percent to thirty percent and higher in future. There will be enhanced provisions of reproductive morbidities and health needs of women beyond the reproductive age of 40. Women's access to healthcare need to be strengthened by ensuring that public hospital is more women friendly and by ensuring that staff has an orientation to gender-sensitivity issues. It recognizes the wide ranging consequences of gender based violence and therefore ensure free healthcare to survivors and victims so that their dignity is maintained.

The Ground Realities: What went wrong?

Shankar and Reddy (2012) in a study exploring prevalence of anemia found that it is high and rising in several states of India. The population is gender biased towards women and the risk of severe anemia is greater among pregnant women. The data gathered from Koppal District of Karnataka shows maternal safety and rights are not fully provided. Women have to go for daily wage labour and have limited access to food. They experience early marriage, repeated pregnancy, inadequate nutrition and so on. The social structure shapes the way families normalize common symptoms of Anemia such as fatigue viewing it as natural consequence of daily work. Narratives from the field reveal the fate of two women from this area. The fate of Renukavva, married women of age 15 years and who got pregnant within a year was death. Shankar and Reddy (2012) narrates,

> When she visited the local primary health centre, the medical officer did not identify her to be at risk but just gave a routine nutritional advice and tablets. But at home her family advised her not to take the tablets (Iron and Folic acid) due to the common belief that these supplement increases babies growth making delivery more difficult. When her hands and fit swelled up her family assumed this as normal in pregnancy. Blood test revealed moderate anemia. Later she developed breathlessness; cough, more swelling and the medical officer recognized severe anemia but attributed her breathlessness to Asthma. Renukavva died of heart failure by the time her family decided to take her to secondary health care facility. The fate of Gowramma was no different. Aged 22 years and with her fourth pregnancy, she was detected with anemia. She was given Iron and Folic acid tablet but she could not take them due to Nausea. Her symptoms became severe. The attending doctor gave her advice but failed to give aggressive treatment. Another frontline health worker recognized her severe condition and advised her to take iron injections but did not refer her to appropriate facility. She gave birth to a girl but then begun to bleed excessively. She needed blood transfusion but there was no stock of blood in the hospital. She died during the journey at another hospital. (p. 67)

It is questioned as to why not the health workers questioned and explore the fact that in spite of tablets being provided to pregnant women, they do not take them out of traditional beliefs. They do not question irrational and ineffective treatment processes. Why they do not create awareness among family members? Anemia cannot be tackled if not there is any food security given to women that will ensure their claim to fair share of food and household resources. Gaitonde (2012) studied to criticize the Pregnancy and Infant Cohort Monitoring and Evaluation system introduced in Tamil Nadu in 2008. The aim of the Pregnancy and Infant Cohort Monitoring and Evaluation system was basically to create a database of currently pregnant women, extent of pregnancy related risk factors, and the need for follow up, immunization and so on. On analysis it is found that the system is too much dependent on information technology for collection of information. It is a total state control determination of the 'right behaviour' and its measurement. From the feminist point of view, it is questioned as to what extent these public health systems improves the women's experience, trust and her goals of equity and emancipation. In this case, what is reported was coercion on women to get registered to the system. There is also increased pressure on health workers to perform. For example, the village health nurse is found to be overburdened enough to commit to her visits and follow ups. They have become dehumanized. According to Gaitonde (2012).

> A woman reported that when the nurse came for routine visit she complained of diarrhoea and asked for help. The nurse replied she is here to fill up forms and dismissed the diarrhoea stating that it is only the baby's hair that is irritating the womb. Women also experienced the victim blaming approach as under such registered health system the patients (victims) are blamed for missing out antenatal visits or for delivering at home. The health workers do not try to tackle the existing structural and social determinants and in providing an overall trust and care for a proper experience of pregnancy. (p. 121)

In the previous section of this chapter NFHS-4 and the general improvement of MMR in India is explored. However, many researchers and stakeholders are not ready to uncritically accept the data provided by NFHS-4. According to Joe, Sharma, Sharma, Shanta, Ramanathan, Mishra and Sri (2015), the focus is laid on MMR across Empower Action Group (EAG). The researchers note that the trends in MMR for the past two decades, especially the rate of decline, do not commensurate well with the observed improvements in the socio-economic indicators of the country. The disparity in intra-state and interstate data is a major policy concern. For example, MMR for EAG in Assam was 438 in 2001-03, 257 in 2010-12 but it is five times higher than that in Kerala (MMR 66). It is also argued by experts that the decline in MMR is only statistically significant for large sample of data. The indirect causes of maternal death are socially significant. These causes are anaemia, hemorrhage, delays in decision making and care seeking at the household level, delays in arranging transport to nearest health facility and not getting appropriate care in health facility.

It is evident that Women's health needs a new approach. Gnanadasan (1986) argues that when analyzing ill health in India, it cannot be seen as an isolated issue separated from other social, political and economic issues. People involved in health movement and women's movement in India realized that the ill health condition of women here is associated with wider context of existing political, economic, and social norms in which the women are second class citizens. Women as a whole needs to be at focal point. Only addressing maternal health will not solve the problem. Female child health need to be monitored, ill health of women due to overwork and lack of facilities for women working in unorganized sector also need to be addressed. The fact that the health system in India is quite profit oriented, can be traced to its root in Colonial period. If a person's health is only seen in the context of the extraction of labour for profit, a denial of justice to a vast majority is inevitable. Joe et. al. (2017) also point out the fact that health system in India is historically grossly neglected. The government has not pursued the egalitarian goals of health rather have emphasized on the utilitarian role of health as an input of economic growth and vice versa instead of seeking health improvements as an end in itself.

Analysis of the Current Situation: Some Theoretical Insights

It is evident that the low, disadvantaged health status of women in India is rooted in their unequal position in patriarchal society in comparison to men. Social determinants of health status are found in variously situated studies. Based on studies conducted in America from 1999 to 2007, Miech, Pampel, Kim and Rogers (2011) proposes that inequality and disparities in socio-economic status is increasing mortality rate. People in lower socio-economic strata are more likely to suffer when new health threats enter a society. They already have poorer health and fewer health reserves to resist the effects of new threats. They have higher levels of unhealthy behaviour like smoking, lack of regular exercise and these amplify the negative effects of the new threats. They are less likely to adapt to new technologies of health that may have protected against new health threats. The health disparities continuously shift. As present disparities lessen, new disparities emerge and widens in outcomes that will be predominant in future. The disparities remain resilient despite policy efforts. The widening emerging disparities play important role in perpetuating of mortality disparities. England (2016) studies class differences in efficacy among young, unmarried women who do not want to get pregnant yet uses contraception inconsistently. According to England (2016),

> Efficacy is conceptualized as including planfulness, selfregulation, assertiveness and beliefs in one's ability to carry out behaviours that will help realize one's goal. Learned efficacy is important mediator through which education encourages multiple behaviours that in turn enhance health. Efficacy caters to a sense of personal control; a belief that one can take action and achieve goals thereby. Low class

background, poverty and uncertainty lower one's self-belief and poverty erodes self-regulation. Thereby efficacy is affected. (p. 2)

Efficacy is thus conceptualized as a skill which is part of learned culture. Here women's choice and decision-making capacity in context of health is indirectly shaped by presence and/or absence of culturally learned efficacy. Identifying and locating gender bias within health system, health policies and health research in a way challenges the widely prevalent bio-medical model that shapes the popular understanding of health. The physical differentiation between women and men, their sexually different existence often lessens the importance of gender as an explanatory factor capable of affecting the health status of women. This foundational implication that there is a distinction between sex and gender within feminist theorization is itself challenged. According to Harrison (2006), feminism has failed to produce a social science that recognizes and understands that biological characteristics are given and a biology that takes full account of the fact that human beings are pre-eminently social and cultural beings who while shaping the world around them, also shape themselves. Humans actively negotiate and shape processes such as representations of their sex. The irony is that the concept of gender has remained tied to the concept of sex. The term gender is often found in composites such as sex/ gender or sex and gender. The notion of sex is problematical, a taken for granted binary division of the population. The notion of sex thrive on the doctrine of natural difference; the conviction of the foundational character of biological difference for gender. This foundational and fundamental difference between sexes is often actively embraced by feminist thinkers as an acknowledgement of the specificity of women's experiences in the flesh. It is assumed that sex has constancy. The apparent reality of sex is strongly associated with the idea that it is the body (sex) that have substance whereas mind and relationship (gender) do not. In her book, *Bodies That Matter* (1993) Judith Butler refer to this as 'materiality of sex' where body is placed as something outside mind, relationship and language (Harrison, 2006, p.37). Gender as an analytical category is brought into visibility in both modern and post modern thinking in somewhat different ways. The modernist approach enables feminists to recognise and name the inconsistent expectations of gender as a problem requiring redress, to seek greater equality and revolutionary transformation in gender order. The postmodernist approach however has nudged the feminists towards taking gender as a verb. According to Butlér (1993) 'to gender' is something one does, something that is done in discourses and material structures (Di Palma and Ferguson, 2006, p. 128). Gender is defined as both the social or cultural organization of sexual difference and as a system of power relations privileging man and masculinity as prior to and more worthy than women and femininity. Gender framed in postmodern terms offers a site from which to problematize the gender categories that modernism produced. Feminists talk of explaining the world by seeking valid and reliable knowledge to represent reality. Postmodern thinkers talk more about understanding the world by uncovering the hidden or distorted behind the surface accounts. Modernist approaches are dependent on stable relations between language and the world that language apprehends whereas postmodern approach problematizes the very representation of the reality. Thus following the postmodernist views, a health system essentially needs the narratives of its clients to be effectively addressing their needs. Thus, women as client to the health system need to voice their experiences and the negotiations they make in order to defy misrepresentation.

Medicalization of women's bodies, especially in regards to their reproductive capacities is a well documented source of social control and disempowerment of women. Women bodies are subjected to medical interventions and designated as sick or diseased in the context of fertility and reproductive issues including abortion, pre-menstrual tensions and menopause. They are the sites in which women both individually and collectively, loose autonomy and power as against medical dominance. According to Rothman (1982), medical intervention and diagnostics during pregnancy, the movement from home to hospital for giving birth, male physicians and increasing exclusion of women midwives from the birthing process are all aspects of women's loss of control over pregnancy and childbirth (Anleu, 2006, p. 360). Infertility is also designated as a condition requiring medical treatment and intervention rather than a social problem stemming from the stigma of childlessness. It is also to be noted in the context of women body that the interest of the women and that of the foetus may not be compatible; an adverse relationship may exist in which the woman become liable for any birth defects or neonatal problems. In this way, she loses control and decision-making capacity over her body. Pre-menstrual Syndromes (PMS) consisting of dizziness, mood swings etc and menopause, both have negative connotation in medical literature. Other causes such as pressures in a woman's life in case of PMS are not explored and menopause is treated as a deficiency disease in requirement of Hormone Replacement Treatment (HRT). HRT in turn can affect women's health; if used extensively it can cause heart attacks and strokes. Anleu (2006) is critical of the generalization regarding women health and the idea that all women will experience certain medically defined conditions due to hormones. Such an idea attributes all conditions to hormones and other factors and social events in women's lives remain unexplored. According to Khanna (2005) the women's health approach is an alternative to biomedical model. Following it, Obstetrics and gynaecology is analyzed from social health and public health perspective; it incorporates women's emotional, social, cultural, spiritual, and physical well being. It recognizes the need for exploring other factors along with biology; it recognizes the validity of life experiences of women, in exploring women's belief about and expectations regarding health. Women have the right to achieve, sustain and maintain health, as defined by herself, to her full potential. Feminists' arguments about abortion also include question of reproductive autonomy or choice. Legalization of abortion does not give absolute right to abortion to the women; it rather allows the medical practitioners to perform abortion under certain circumstances. Though abortion is a medically safe procedure, it has effect on emotional health. On the other hand, research shows that when women opt for abortion by choice there are positive emotional and health outcomes. There is a sense of personal empowerment as well as educational, economical and social outcomes for women (Lamanna, Reidmann and Strahm, 2009, p. 239).

Gender bias and disadvantaged status of women in society can be countered through the process of gender mainstreaming. Gender mainstreaming in health sector has been pointed as early as 1970s to ensure women's share of gain in overall development. Gender mainstreaming is defined by UN Economic and Social Council as the process of assessing the implications for women and men of any planned actions, legislations, policies and programmes in all areas and at all levels (Ravindran and Kelkar-Khambete, 2008, p.123). It is strategy to make women's and men's concerns and experiences an integral dimension of designs, implementation, monitoring and evaluation of policies and programmes in all political, economic and societal sphere so that women and men can benefit equally and inequality is not perpetuated. The ultimate end is to attain gender equality. Two dimensions of gender mainstreaming are

(i) operational mainstreaming refers to integration of equality concerns into the content of policies, projects and programs to ensure positive impacts on women and to reduce gender inequalities;

(ii) institutional mainstreaming refers to the addressing of internal dynamics of formal and informal institutions such goals agenda setting, governance and procedures related to day to day functioning to promote gender equality. An example of gender mainstreaming in health programs is cited in Woman Centered Health Project under Mumbai Municipality in collaboration with SAHAJ in 2002. The unique process involved implementation of reproductive health services that are closer to women. It involved men so that they do not get to show control over women. It stressed on women friendly procedures and improved provider-client communication. Quality of care assured the maintenance of respect and privacy of women while being physically examined, assured presence of lady physician and held gender sensitization workshop for providers and managers. Integration of gender in health research is also cited as a significant step towards gender mainstreaming. The challenges facing gender mainstreaming to the health sector is also manifold. The health needs and experiences of women and men being different; this biological difference is attributed in each aspects of health. Addressing maternal health is regarded as sufficient and gender issues in other health problems are not explored. The health data is bit complex, but is understood simplistically. Given that mortality rate among men is higher to that of women; in general, for many stakeholders gender mainstreaming is not necessary. They remain unconvinced of gender based inequalities in health sectors such as the rate of maternal morbidity and limited access to healthcare. Again the bio-medical approach to health as widely prevalent it is, fails to understand the social dimensions and determinants of health. Healthcare professionals mostly consider themselves as gender neutral, and the see gender mainstreaming as a diversion from actual issues, time and resources.

Conclusion: A Call for Women's Agency

Determining health status, as is seen through above analysis is an exercise that needs in-depth understanding of the various factors, structures and agencies involved in the immediate context. Though analytical studies always aspire to chalk out few generalized insights, in actuality, the ground realities are so complex and dynamic that any rigid, fixed understanding can only be incomplete and limiting in true sense. The above discussion lays a great emphasis on agency than on structures and systems. The experience and narratives of the stakeholders, especially the clients (women) ideally should shape the healthcare system. The power to choose, control and decide should lie with them. But to choose and decide, the women need to be aware, because decision-making for development should be informed decision-making. Also the awareness created should be culturally relevant, scientifically accurate, non-judgmental and unbiased. Edmunds and Gupta (2016) focuses on few NGOs and stakeholders in Delhi who in order to tackle VAW, IPV that is affecting human rights and health status of women, took to the promotion of sexuality education to serve both adolescents and adults. Sexuality education can prevent gender violence by building essential life skills such as decision –making skills, refusal skills, it builds up the capacity to understand consensus, it provides essential understanding of SRH, it helps to recognize and report violence and abuse. The focus is also laid on consensual sex as an alternative to coercion. Scholars and advocates are increasingly addressing issues of women sexual pleasure, consent and agency. They are exploring the history of sexual repression in South Asia. It is argued that patriarchal norms, colonial rule and nationalist projects have actually silenced female sexual expression, certain kinship practices and liberal gender norms. Instead of focusing on agency, development practitioners focused more on medicalized, negative and dangerous aspects such as population control, sexually transmitted diseases and sexual violence. It is therefore essential to hear women's narratives and experiences. Agency being the ability to define one's goal and act upon it; it includes the meaning, motivation and purpose which the individual bring to the activity; it can take the form of bargaining and negotiation, subversion and resistance, reflections and analysis.

References

- Allendorf, Keera (2013). Going Nuclear? Family Structure and Young Women's Health in India, 1992-2006. *Demography, 50(3),* 853-880.
- Anleu, Sharyn Roach (2006) Gendered Bodies: Between Conformity and Autonomy, In Kathy Davis, Mary Evans and Judith Lorber (Eds.), *Handbook of Gender and Women's Studies*,(pp.357-375) London, Sage.
- Bean, Susan. S (1981) Towards a Semiotics of "Purity" and "Pollution" in India, *American Ethnologist, Vol 8, No.3*, 575-595.
- Edmunds Emme and Ankit Gupta (2016) Headline Violence and Silenced Pleasure: Contested framings of consensual sex, power and rape in Delhi, India 2011-2014, *Reproductive Health Matters, Vol 24, No 47*,126-140.
- England, Paula (2016) Sometimes the Social Becomes The Personal: Gender, Class and Sexualities. *American Sociological Review, Vol 81(1),* 4-28.
- Di Palma, Carolyn, Kathy E Ferguson (2006) Clearing Grounds and Making Connections: Modernism, Postmodernism, Feminism, In Kathy Davis, Mary Evans and Judith Lorber (Eds.). *Handbook of Gender and Women's Studies*, (pp.127-145), London, Sage.
- Gaitonde, Rakhal (2012) Registration and Monitoring of pregnant women in Tamil Nadu: A critique, *Reproductive Health Matters, Vol 20, No.39*, 118-129.
- Gnanadason, Aruna (1986) Women's Health: Plea for a New Approach, Economic *and Political Weekly, Vol. 21, No. 37*, 1630-1632.

- Harrison, Wendy Cealey (2006) The Shadow and The Substance: The Sex/ Gender Debate, In Kathy Davis, Mary Evans and Judith Lorber (Eds.). *Handbook of Gender and Women's Studies*, (pp.35-52), London, Sage.
- International Institute for Population Sciences (IIPS) and ICF (2017) *National Family Health Survey (NFHS-4), 2015-16: India.* Mumbai: IIPS. (Retrieved on 19.10.19) http://rchiips.org/NFHS/factsheet_NFHS-4. shtml.
- Joe William, Suresh Sharma, Jyotsna Sharma, Y Manasa Shanta, Mala Ramanathan, Udaya Shankar Mishra and B. Subha Sri (2015) Maternal Mortality in India: A Renew of Trends and Pattern, *IEG Working Paper No. 353.*
- Kamalapur, Sunilkumar M and Somanath Reddy (2013) Women Health in India: An Analysis. *International Research Journal in Social Sciences, Vol 2(10).*
- Khanna, Renu (2005) Obstetrics and Gynaecology: A Women's Health Approach to Textbooks. *Economic and Political Weekly. Vol.40, No. 18.* 1876-1881.
- Lamanna, Mary Ann, Agnes Reidmann, Ann Strahm (2009) *Making Choice in a Diverse Society*. USA. Wadsworth. Cengage Learning.
- Ma, Sai and Neeraj Sood (2008) A Comparison of Health Systems in China and India. *Occasional Paper Series*, Rand Corporation. (Retrieved on 19.10.19) https://www.rand.org/content/dam/rand/pubs/occasional_ papers/2008/ RAND_OP212.pdf.
- Miech, Richard, Fred Pampel, Jinyoung Kim and Richard G. Rogers (2011) The Enduring Association Between Education and Mortality: The Role of Widening and Narrowing Disparities. *American Sociological Review, 76 (6),* 913-934.
- Ministry of Health and Family Welfare, Government of India (2017) *National Health Policy*. Author. (Retrieved on 29.9.19) https://mohfw.gov. in/sites/default/ files/9147562941489753121.pdf
- National Crime Records Bureau (2017) *Crimes in India 2017*. Author. (Retrieved on 29.9.19) http://ncrb.gov.in/.
- Office of the United Nations High Commissioner for Human Rights and World Health Organization (2008) *The Right to health: Fact Sheet No 31*. United Nations, Geneva. Author. (Retrieved on 28.10.2019) www.ohchr. com
- Ramalingaswami, Prabha (1987) Women's Access to Health care, *Economic and Political Weekly*, Vol22, No.27, 1075-1076.
- Ravindran, TK Sundari and Aarti Kelkar-Khambete (2008) Gender mainstreaming in health: looking back, looking forward, *Global Public Health, 3 (S1),* 121-142.
- Seltzer, Judith R. (2002) *The Origin And Evolution of Family Planning Programme in Developing Countries.* USA. Rand Corporation.
- Shankar, Mridula and Bhavya Reddy (2012) Anaemia in pregnancy still a major cause of morbidity and mortality: insights from Koppal district, Karnataka, India *Reproductive Health Matters, Vol. 20, No. 40*, Sexual, 67-68.
- The George Institute of Global Health India (2016) *Framing Women's Health Issues in 21st Century India- A Policy Report*. New Delhi. Author. (Retrieved on 30.09.19) https://www.georgeinstitute.org/sites/default/files/ framing-womens-health-issues-in-21st-century-india.pdf

- Velkoff, Victoria A and Arjun Adlakha (1998) *Women's Health in India*. U.S Department of Commerce, Economics and Statistics Administration, Bureau of Census. (Retrieved on 30.09.19) https://www.census.gov/ content/dam/Census/ library/publications/1998/demo/wid98-3.pdf.
- Visaria Leela, Shireen Jejeebhoy and Tom Merrick (1999) From Family Planning to Reproductive Health: Challenges Facing India, *International Family Planning Perspectives*, *Vol 25,*S44- S49.
- World Bank (1996) *India: Issues in Women's Health*, Population and Human Resource Operation Division. Author. (Retrieved on 1.10.19.) http:// documents.worldbank.org/curated/en/440921468771644683/pdf/ multi0page.pdf

Notes

1. A life threatening condition caused by body's reaction to an infection.
2. According to Bean (1981), anthropological Research shows that a great deal of activity centres on concern with ritual/religious purity and pollution in India; important rites of passage, such as birth and deaths are organized around management of pollution.
3. Intrauterine device, a contraceptive T-shaped device entered into woman's uterus to prevent pregnancy.
4. Maternal Mortality Ratio is the number of deaths from pregnancy related causes per 100,000 live births. According to World Health Organization, maternal mortality refers to death of a woman while pregnant or within 42 days of termination of pregnancy, caused by pregnancy related issue but not by accident.
5. Related by blood
6. "Maternal Mortality Ratio Down By 37 Points In 3 Years: Health Minister J P Nadda"; Dated 12.06.18. https://www.ndtv.com/indianews/ health-minister-jp-nadda-maternal-mortality-rate-down-by-37- points-in-3-years-1866247.
7. Office of the United Nations High Commissioner for Human Rights
8. The strategy by India introduced in 2014: Reproductive, Maternal, Newborn, Child and Adolescent Health.

3

Addressing Malnutrition among Women and Children in the Developed and Developing States: What Can We Learn?

— *Dr. Tanushree Paul*

Introduction

Nutrition is fast emerging as a development obstacle. To the extent that the "political urgency" of nutrition has the United Nations declare 2016-2025 as the UN Decade of Action on Nutrition with specific nutrition goals to be achieved by the countries across the world by 2025. Initially there was little recognition of prioritising actions to address nutrition, however research done by a group of scientists led by Robert E Black from Johns Hopkins Bloomberg School of Public Health (known as the Maternal and Child Nutrition Study Group) brought concerns about nutrition to the fore (Horton and Lo 2013). Based on their data analysis of 34 countries across Africa, Asia, and the Middle East, accounting for 90 percent of the global burden of under nutrition, they observe that the first 1000 days from conception to 2 years is the critical window of opportunity for addressing malnutrition. "What goes right and what goes wrong for fetal and child nutrition during this period has lasting and irreversible consequences for later life" (Horton and Lo 2013: 1). "If maternal and child nutrition is optimised, the benefits will accrue and extend over several generations" (Ibid).

It needs to be emphasized that malnutrition is as much a problem of men as much it is of women. For example, according to the Comprehensive National Nutrition Survey (2016-2018), the share of boys under 5 years of age who are stunted is 35.4 percent compared to 34 percent of their female counterparts; the corresponding figures for wasting (weight-for-height) are 13.4 and 12.9 percent respectively. Among the adolescents aged 10-19 years, about 29.4 per cent boys and 18.9 percent girls have moderate or severely thin (Body Mass Index for age) in India. Again, about 41 per cent of both boys and girls under 5 years of age suffer from anemia, although the share of adolescent girls (10-19 years of age) was significantly higher, about 39.5 percent compared to adolescent boys, about 17.5 percent. However, given that the first thousand days from conception to two years after birth is being increasingly identified as the critical window of opportunity for addressing malnutrition, the focus of most of nutrition interventions is on women. It has also been argued with compelling evidence that meeting the nutrition deficiencies of adolescent girls yields far-reaching positive effects. Hence this paper primarily focuses on adult and adolescent women and children.

Located in this context, the primary objectives of this paper are: first, to explore to what extent India (vis-à-vis other South Asian countries) and the different States have been able to address malnutrition; and second, to understand the factors/interventions, targeted during the 1000-day period, which are effective in specific contexts to reduce malnutrition vis-à-vis other contexts-an extremely pertinent question for policy analysis as well. This chapter is organized into six sections. This introductory section is followed by a discussion on the data and methods. The third section presents the positioning of India vis-à-vis other South Asian countries in terms of malnutrition parameters. The fourth section portrays the spatial variation of nutritional outcomes in the country. The fifth section presents a comparative analysis of selected Indian states with varying degrees of economic prosperity and nutritional outcomes to understand the drivers of positive change. The concluding section presents policy implications.

Data and Methods

One of the largest databases for nutrition in India is the National Family and Health Survey (NFHS) from which the data for this paper has been primarily extracted. Other sources include: the Global Nutrition Report 2018; Comprehensive National Nutrition Survey 2018, Ministry of Health and Family Welfare, Government of India.

Before proceeding with data analysis, the selection of indicators must be clearly spelled out. As mentioned earlier, women and men have different experiences of nutrition. The indicators for exploring the nutrition outcomes are based on those from the 2025 Global Nutrition targets (World Health

Organisation and UNICEF 2017) and include: under-5 stunting, under-5 wasting, low birth weight among under-5 for the children; prevalence of anaemia among women of reproductive age, both pregnant and non-pregnant, and adult overweight or obesity (BMI>= 25kg/m2). The proximate determinants that influence nutrition during the 1000-day period have been selected on the basis of an extensive review of literature as well as the identified nutrition-specific and nutrition sensitive indicators by the UNICEF and the WHO. These determinants cover the following domains: Infant and Young Child Feeding Practices (IYCF), Micronutrient Supplementation, mother and child care related factors and utilization of associated services, over-all health related factors, nutrition information.

India in the context of South Asia

The recent release of the Global Hunger Index 2019 and the observed downward-slipping of India's rank vis-à-vis other South Asian countries (102 out of 117 counties world over) probably is indicative of the dismal nutrition scenario in the country. According to the Global Nutrition Report 2018, among all the regions of the world, South Asia bears the highest burden of stunting with about 38.9 percent of the worlds stunted under-5 children living here. Although stunting among children in Asia has declined to 23.2% from 38.1% since 2000, yet the situation is considerably grim, when compared to other developing regions of the world. As of 2015, about 37.9 per cent of the under-five children are stunted as against a global average of 22.2 percent while the averages for whole of Asia and Africa are 23.2 per cent and 30.3 percent respectively. About 26.9 million out of total 50.5 million wasted children under 5 children are wasted as against the developing country average of 8.9 percent and global average of 7.5 per cent in 2017.

At the disaggregated level, two of the South Asian countries, India (46.6 million) and Pakistan (10.7 million) along with Nigeria (13.9 million) are home to almost half (47.2%) of all stunted children in the world. On the other hand, India (25.5 million) is also one of the countries along with Nigeria (3.4 million) and Indonesia (3.3 million) which contribute to the highest share of wasted children under 5 years of age. Further, although overweight and obesity are typical problems of the upper-middle income countries, India and Pakistan are among the South Asian countries that are home to more than a million overweight children, the other countries being China, Indonesia, Egypt and Brazil. This indicates a dual burden of malnutrition in our country.

Table 3.1: Nutrition Indicators* in South Asia

			Child (under-five) nutrition status				Child and adolescent (aged 5-19) nutrition status				Adult nutrition status					Infant and young child feeding practices			
			Stunting		*Wasting*		*Under-weight*		*Over weight*		*Obesity among adults*		*Anaemia*			*Exclusive breastfeeding till 6 months*		*Minimum acceptable diet*	
India	5865.35	No data	37.9		19.8	21.7	50.1	58.1	6.1	7.5	5.1	2.7	50.1	51.5	51.4	53.6	56	9.7	9.4
Bangladesh	3409.02	27.8	35.5	36.8	13.6	15.1	40.2	50.7	8.7	9.3	5	2.3	45.7	39.6	39.9	55.5	55.1	23	22.7
Pakistan	4608.88	No data	37.1	38.2	6.6	7.6	41.6	51.0	9.1	10.1	11.3	6	51.3	52.2	52.1	43.7	50.6	13.2	12.2
Sri Lanka	11079.71	15.9	17.3		15.1		35	40.4	11.7	13.9	7.3	2.9	35.4	32.5	32.6	82		No data	
Nepal	2314.28	21.8	35.8	36.2	9.9	9.4	36.2	50.9	7.8	7.2	5.4	2.7	40.0	34.9	35.1	63.9	66.3	37.3	34.3
Bhutan	7299.2	11.7	33.6	33.4	5.5	6.2	38.1	48.5	9.5	10.8	8.5	4.7	32.8	35.7	35.6	51.4		No data	
South Asia	5890.02	27.25	37.22	38.09	17.4	19.2							48.62	49.01	48.95	53.3	54.5	11.94	11.96

*Indicators are selected on the basis of 2025 Global Nutrition Targets

Italicised figures indicate national averages due to absence of gender segregated data

India- Under-5 stunting and wasting for the year 2015, Child and adolescent (aged 5-19) nutrition status and adult nutrition status for the year 2016, Infant and young child feeding practices for the year 2015.

Bangladesh- Under-5 stunting and wasting for the year 2014, Child and adolescent (aged 5-19) nutrition status and adult nutrition status for the year 2016, Infant and young child feeding practices for the year 2014.

Pakistan- Under-5 stunting and wasting for the year 2018, Child and adolescent (aged 5-19) nutrition status and adult nutrition status for the year 2016, Infant and young child feeding practices for the year 2018.

Bhutan- Under-5 stunting and wasting for the year 2010, Child and adolescent (aged 5-19) nutrition status and adult nutrition status for the year 2016, Infant and young child feeding practices for the year 2015.

Sri Lanka- All indicators are for the year 2016.

Nepal- All indicators are for the year 2016.

South Asia- Stunting for the year 2016, Wasting for the year 2018, Infant and young child feeding practices for the year 2016.

Source: Global Nutrition Report, 2018.

Table-3.1 clearly indicates that despite having the second highest GDP per capita adjusted to PPP in 2015, India fared miserably in almost all indicators of malnutrition, except obesity and overweight. Particularly worth mentioning is that India was home to the highest percentage of under-5 stunted and wasted children and underweight adolescents (both male and female) as well as the second highest percentage of women suffering from anemia (both pregnant and non-pregnant), after Pakistan. Less than 10 percent of the infant and young children had access to minimum acceptable diet, the lowest among all South Asian countries. Nepal and Bangladesh with much lower GDP per capita adjusted to PPP fared much better than all South Asian countries average taken together and India in particular.

Table-3.2 also indicates that the burden of malnutrition is experienced differently by women and men. The proportion of boys suffering from stunting and wasting as well as underweight is slightly higher compared to girls, however, the problem of obesity appears to be a problem among adult women across all countries. Anemia, a well-known condition of malnutrition, continues to hold a high prevalence in South Asia in general and India in particular, with nearly half the women suffering from it, the proportion of non-pregnant women being slightly higher compared to their pregnant counterparts. In fact, the share of the latter suffering from anemia is on the rise globally, it has increased from 31.1% to 32.5% between 2000 and 2016. Among the pregnant women, the corresponding share has decreased marginally from 32.8 to 31.6 percentage during the same period.

It is quite evident that Bangladesh and Nepal, have managed to perform much better at lower levels of GDP per capita economic compared to other South Asian countries, particularly India. The nutrition programs in Bangladesh such as the Strengthening Household Ability to Respond to Development Opportunities (SHOUHARDO) project, the Alive and Thrive (A & T) project1 in Bangladesh and so forth adopted a cross-sectoral approach, including Water and Sanitation Hygiene (WASH) and health related interventions, which could be a major reason behind its considerable success (https://apps.who.int/iris/bitstream/handle/10665/193991/9789241565 103_eng.pdf). A unique feature of the nutrition interventions of the country include the robustness of the national media campaigns which targeted behaviour change communication as well as fostering proper Infant and IYCF and hygiene, particularly handwashing (see USAID 2015, WHO et al 2015). Nepal, the fifth country to join the Scaling Up Nutrition (SUN) Movement, also succeeded in reducing malnutrition considerably by adopting a multisectoral approach and addressing both nutrition-specific and nutrition-sensitive sectors (health, education, governance, WASH and Agriculture). Here, the Government officials, development partners, academia and independent sector experts joined hands to identify the best practices by reviewing global and national evidences. The Multisector Nutrition Plan (MSNP) was developed by the Government, with five year plans (2013-2017) and ten-year visions (to 2022) (Government of Nepal, 2012). The second phase, MSNP –II (2018-2022) was launched in 2017 targeting children, adolescent girls and women in the country. Various other development partners have joined hands with the national Government to implement MSNP2 (UNICEF 2013). That said, the next section will look into the Indian scenario.

Spatio-Temporal Pattern of Nutrition Outcomes

India is a vast country with great diversities. The national average presented earlier gives only a cursory picture and masks the large differences in nutritional outcomes achieved by the different States. This part of the analysis would be based on the following classification of the States: Empowered Action Group (EAG) States and Non-Empowered Action Group States (Non-EAG States).

Nutritional Status of under-five children

Stunting or height-for-age is an important indicator of malnutrition. Figure 3.1a indicates that among the eight EAG states, five states namely Bihar, UP, Jharkhand, MP and Rajasthan have highest incidence of stunting among children. Chattisgarh is just below India average. It is important to note that the only other State which ranks above India average, along with the EAG States is Gujarat. In other developed states like Maharashtra, Karnataka, Haryana, more than one-third of the under-five children are stunted. Kerala has the lowest incidence of stunting. However, it is heartening to note that although Chattisgarh and UP have the highest incidence of stunting, both the states have experienced considerable decline over the last decade (2005-06 to 2015-16) with the decline being highest in Chattisgarh, about 16 percentage points. Other EAG states which experienced declines higher than India average are Odisha and Uttarakhand. Bihar and Jharkhand experienced very low decline. Among the developed states, Maharashtra, Gujarat, Punjab and Haryana also experienced considerable decline in stunting. The North Eastern States, except Assam, have comparatively lower incidence of stunting and have also done remarkably well in reducing the same.

Wasting or weight-for-height is another important indicator. Figure 3.2a reveals that among the EAG stats, Jharkhand (highest incidence), followed by MP, Chattisgarh and Rajasthan have higher incidence of wasting. Gujarat, interestingly, holds the second highest rank and Maharashtra holds the fifth highest rank in terms of wasting. Kerala, one of the most developed states of India, have higher incidence compared to states like Punjab, Himachal Pradesh and other smaller NE states. Figure 3.2b indicates, and what could be a matter of concern is that, the incidence of stunting is increasing among most of the developed States with the highest being in Maharashtra, followed by Karnataka, Goa, Gujarat, Punjab and Haryana. Kerala experienced a nominal decline. The incidence of wasting is also increasing in the EAG states, except MP, Bihar and Jharkhand, albeit at a slower pace compared to the developed states.

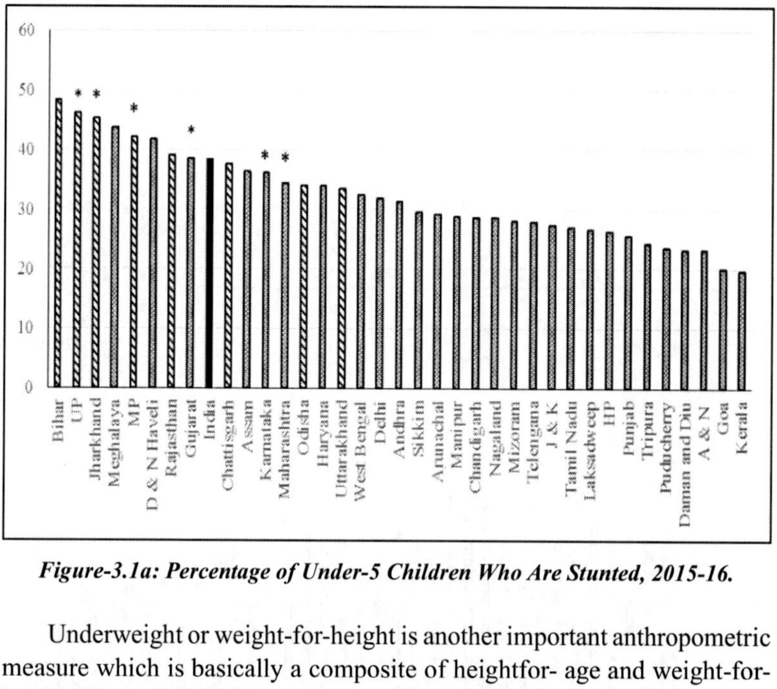

Figure-3.1a: Percentage of Under-5 Children Who Are Stunted, 2015-16.

Underweight or weight-for-height is another important anthropometric measure which is basically a composite of heightfor- age and weight-for-height. Figure 3.3a indicates that not only in all the EAG states but also in Gujarat and Maharashtra, the prevalence of underweight children is higher than India average. In Kerala it is less than 20 percent while in Punjab and Himachal Pradesh, it is slightly above 20 percent. In Haryana, it is nearly 30 percent. Karnataka and Andhra Pradesh are close to national average. It is the lowest in Mizoram followed by Manipur and Kerala. Fortunately, all

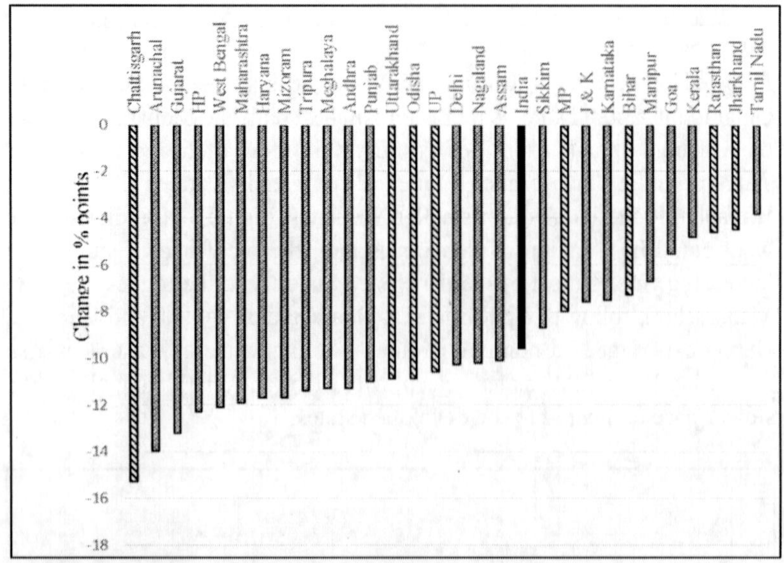

Hatched Bars represent Empowered Action Group States Starred
Bars represent states having dedicated nutrition missions
Change in percentage graphs exclude all UTs and Telengana due to no data in NFHS 3 *Source:* Author's construction from NFHS 4 data

Figure-3.1b: Change between 2015-16 and 2005-06.

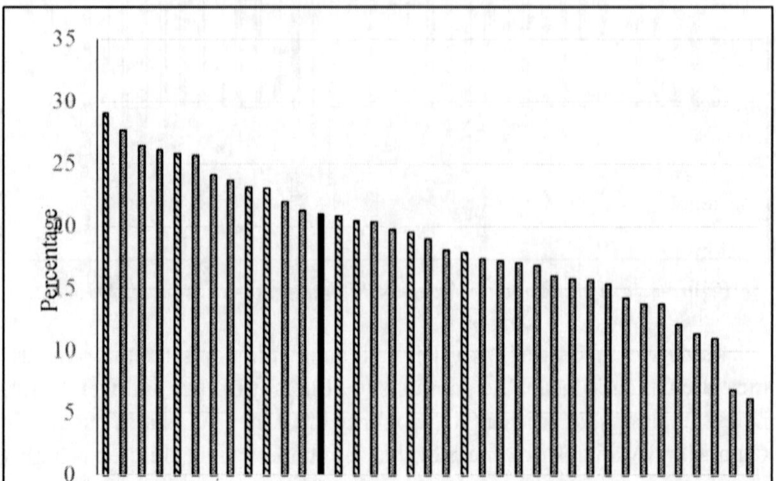

Figure-3.2a: Percentage of Under-5 Children Who Are Wasted, 2015-16.

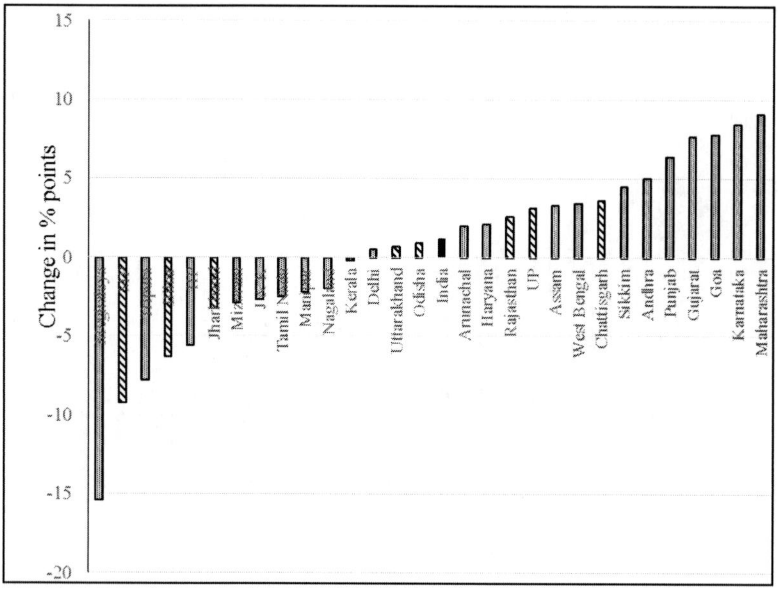

Hatched Bars represent Empowered Action Group States

Change in percentage graphs exclude all UTs and Telengana due to no data in NFHS 3 *Source:* Author's construction from NFHS 4data

Figure-3.2b: Change between 2015-16 and 2005-06.

the EAG states experienced considerable decline between 2005-06 and 2015-16 except UP and Rajasthan, the highest decline being in Meghalaya followed by MP (more than 15 percentage point drop). Among the developed States, Maharashtra, Gujarat and Punjab (about 5 percentage points and less) experienced low decline, much below India average. Haryana experienced a decline of about 10 percentage points (Figure-3.3b).

Among the children under 5 suffering from anemia, Haryana ranks first among the States followed by Jharkhand and both the States experienced very low decline between 2005-06 and 2015-16 as well. Gujarat ranks sixth with more than 60 percent of its under-5 children suffering from anemia, much above India average and also experienced very low decline (ranking 12th), below India average. Although all the EAG states, except Chattisgarh and Odisha, had very high incidence of anemia among children, they have also performed remarkably well in terms of reducing the same. The highest decline has taken place in Assam followed by Chhattisgarh, to the order of greater than 30 per cent. In Uttarakhand, MP, Rajasthan, the decline has been slower, below India average. Interestingly, in Goa and Delhi, it has increased. Tamil Nadu had about 50 percent of its

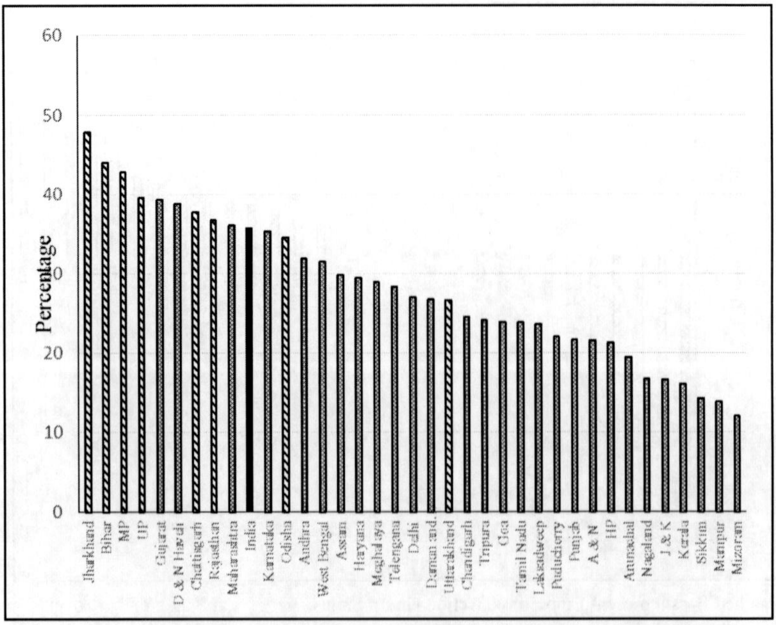

Figure-3.3a: Percentage of Under-5 Children Who Are Underweight

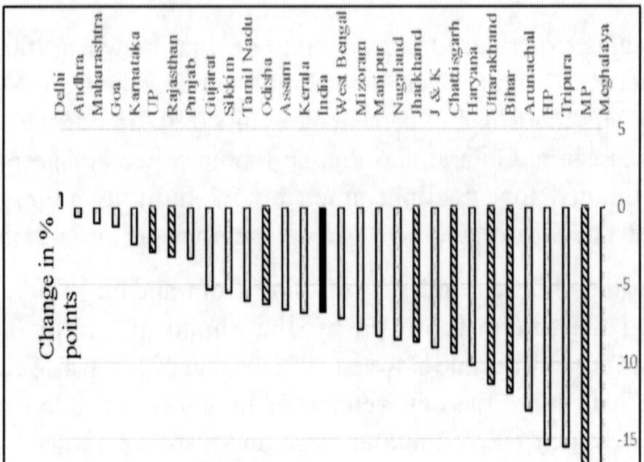

Hatched Bars represent Empowered Action Group States
Change in percentage graphs exclude all UTs and Telengana due to no data in NFHS 3 *Source:* Author's construction from NFHS 4data

Figure-3.3b: Change between 2015-16 and 2005-06.

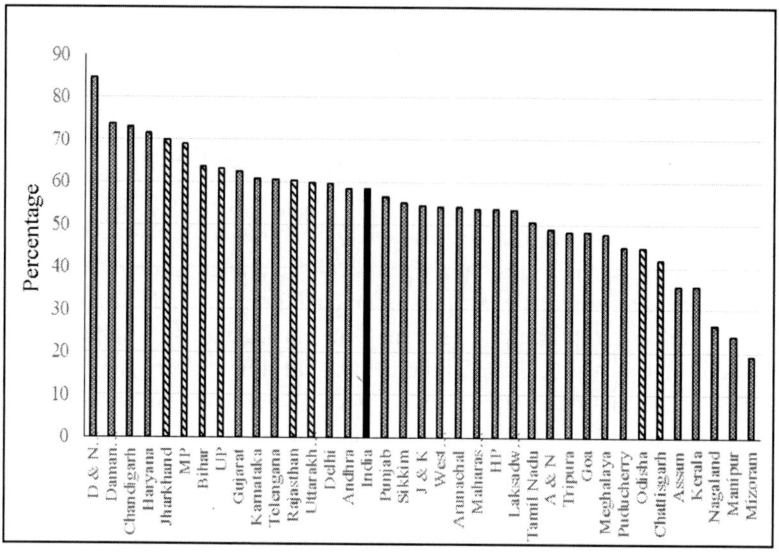

Figure-3.4a: Percentage of Under-5 Children Who Have Anemia.

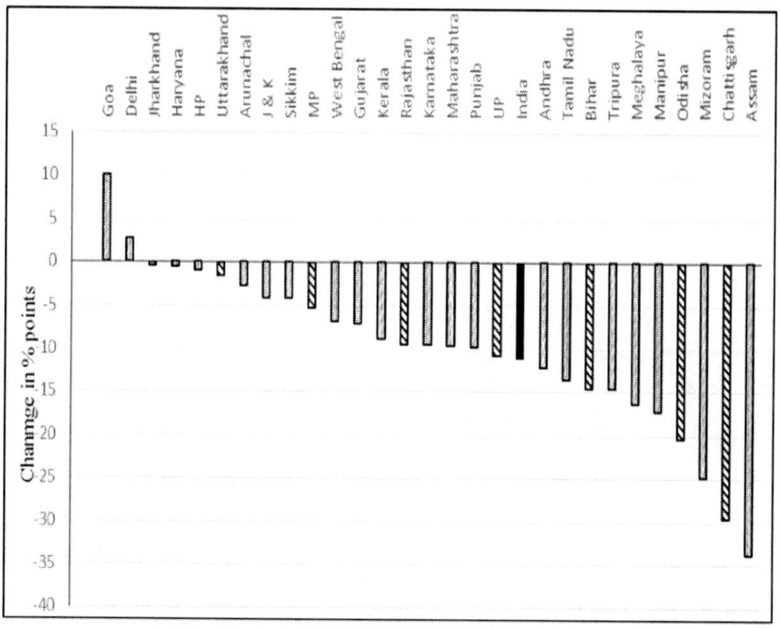

Hatched Bars represent Empowered Action Group States

Change in percentage graphs exclude all UTs, Nagaland and Telengana due to no data in NFHS 3

Source: Author's construction from NFHS-4 data

Figure-3.4b: Change between 2015-16 and 2005-06.

under-5 children as anemic and yet the decline in the State has been lower than some of the States having higher incidence such as Bihar as well as lower incidence such as Chhattisgarh and Odisha (Figures-3.4a and 3.4b).

Nutritional Status among Adult Women, 15-49 Age Group

In terms of percentage of adult women of the reproductive age group who are severely underweight, Gujarat ranks one followed by the EAG states of Jharkhand, Bihar, Rajasthan, MP and Odisha. Maharashtra ranks eight, above India average. In Punjab, Himachal Pradesh and Haryana the proportion is less than eight per cent while in Kerala and smaller North Eastern States, it is less than four percent. In terms of decline between 2005-06 and 2015-16, Tripura ranks one followed by Chhattisgarh and West Bengal (greater than eight percentage points). In Gujarat the decline is by about five percentage points, below national average. There has been a slight increase in the proportion of underweight women in Delhi (Figures 3.5a and 3.5b). It is alarming indeed that the proportion of women in the reproductive age group who are either overweight or obese is rising in all the states. It is worth noting that this proportion is not only higher among the relatively developed states vis-à-vis the EAG states, but also increasing considerably among the former compared to the latter, except Kerala. Andhra Pradesh and Kerala have the highest incidence

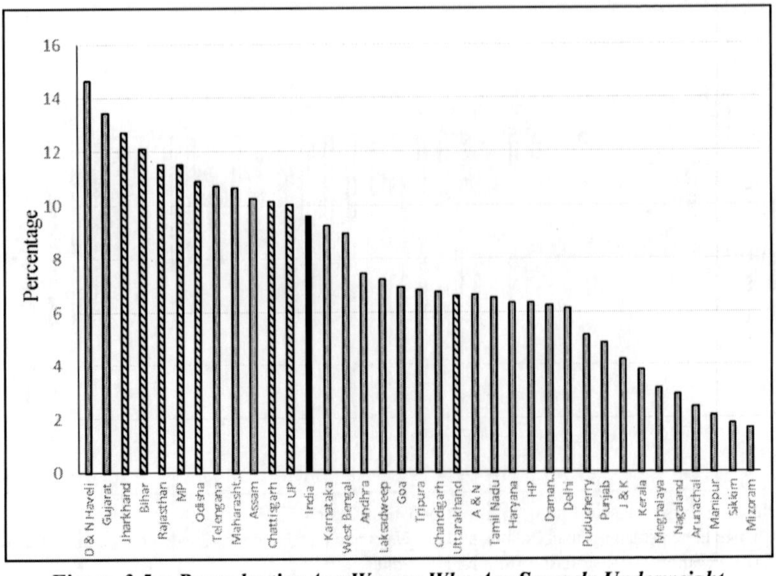

Figure-3.5a: Reproductive Age Women Who Are Severely Underweight.

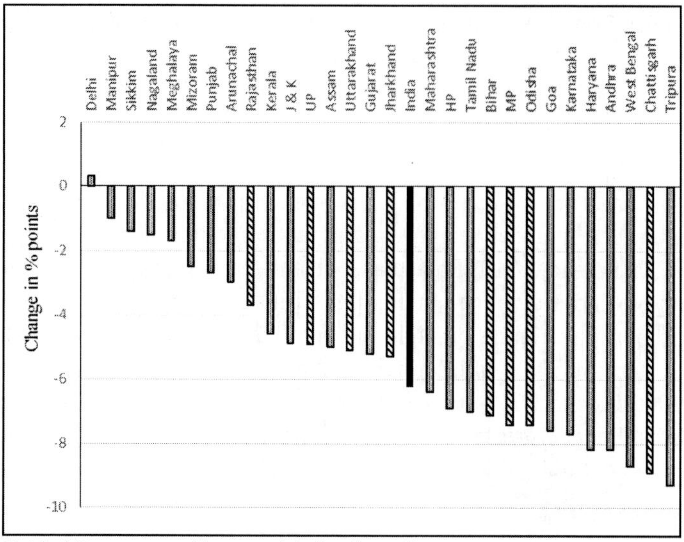

Hatched Bars represent Empowered Action Group States
Change in percentage graphs exclude all UTs and Telangana due to no data in NFHS 3
Source: Author's construction from NFHS-4 data

Figure-3.5b: Change between 2015-16 and 2005-06.

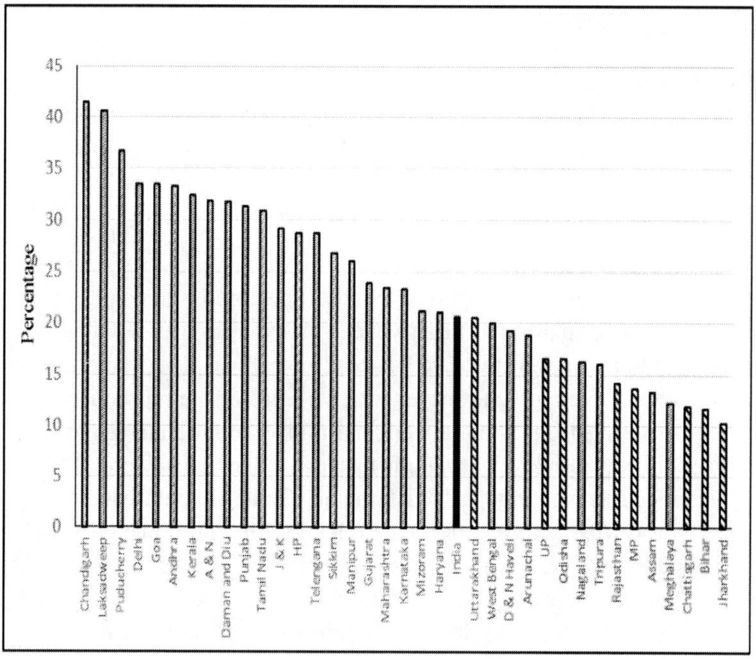

Figure-3.6a: Reproductive Age Women Who Are Either Overweight or Obese, 2015-16.

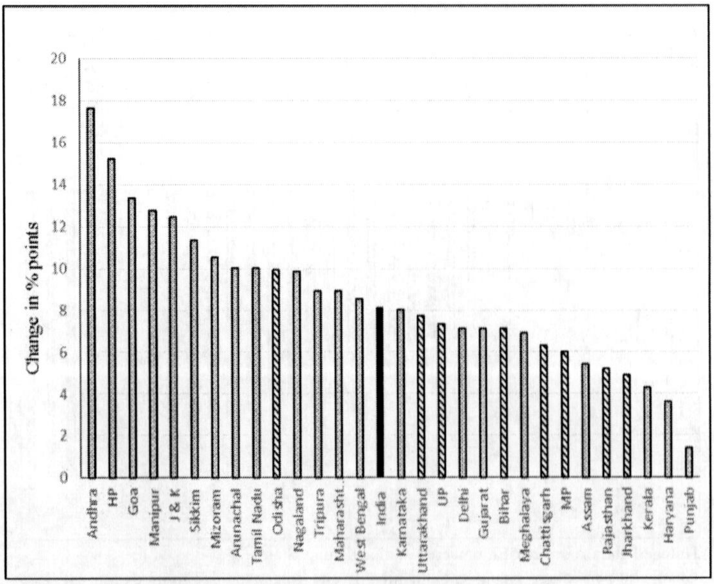

Hatched Bars represent Empowered Action Group States
Change in percentage graphs excludes all UTs and Telengana due to no data in NFHS 3
Source: Author's construction from NFHS 4data

Figure-3.6b: Change between 2015-16 and 2005-06.

percentage of overweight or obese women followed by Punjab and Tamil Nadu. Gujarat, Maharashtra and Haryana also have high shares, those above national average. Lowest percentage is observed in Jharkhand followed by Bihar and Chhattisgarh. In terms of change, the increase has been lower than national average in all the EAG states except Odisha (Figures 3.6a and 3.6b).

Anemia among women of reproductive age group is a major nutrition related concern as it also has negative impact upon the health and nutrition of the children. Among the EAG states, only Bihar and Jharkhand are above national average with more than two-third of the reproductive age women suffering from anemia. Haryana ranks second among the States while Tamil Nadu ranks eighth. Punjab is just above India average. Among the developed States, only Maharashtra and Kerala are below the national average. And what is more alarming is that the share has increased in the last ten years in nine states, highest being in Punjab and Haryana ranks fifth in terms of increase. It has decreased in all the EAG states except UP, the highest decrease being in Sikkim followed by Assam (Figures 3.7a and 3.7b).

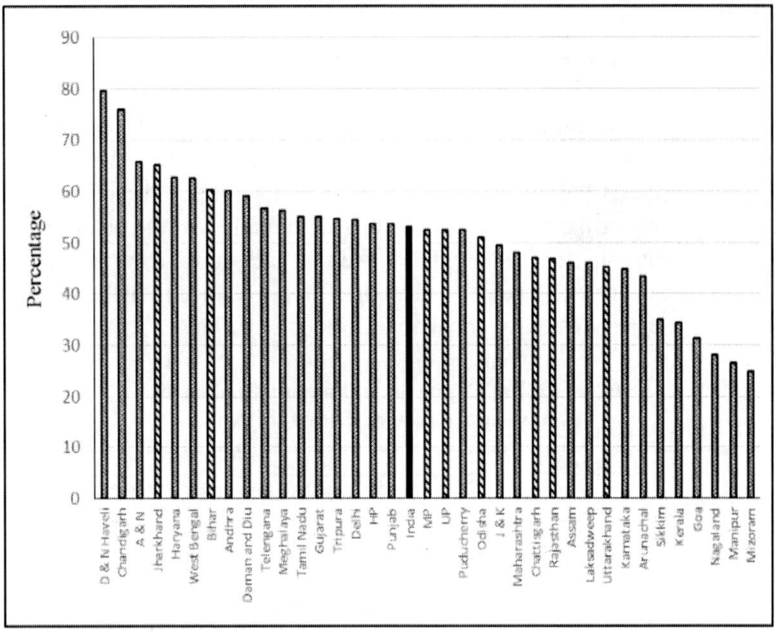

Figure-3.7a: Reproductive Age Women Who Have Anemia, 2015-16.

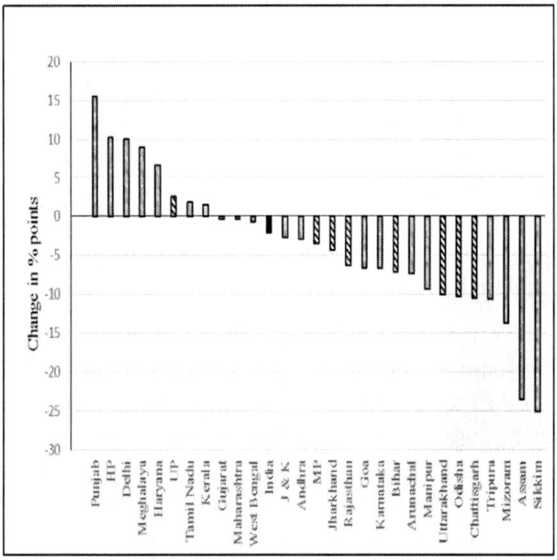

Hatched Bars represent Empowered Action Group States
Change in percentage graphs excludes all UTs, Nagaland and Telangana due to no data in NFHS-3
Source: Author's construction from NFHS-4 data

Figure-3.7b: Change between 2015-16 and 2005-06.

Economic prosperity and malnutrition:

The States marked in bold letters are EAG States while those marked in bold and italicized are the developed States with poor nutritional outcomes. It is evident that during 2015-16, the per capita SDP in Haryana and Maharashtra as well as Gujarat are even higher than Kerala. Yet, as the preceding discussion revealed, the nutritional outcomes in these States in terms of most of the parameters is rather deplorable. On the other hand, the EAG States, understandably fall in the first and second quartile classes i.e. low per capita SDP as well as having high prevalence of malnutrition, yet their progress in addressing malnutrition is remarkable.

Table-3.2: Per Capita State Domestic Product at Factor Cost (Constant Prices), 2015-16

Quartile classes	*States*
Fourth Quartile (Greater than 1,20,684)	Goa, Delhi, Chandigarh, Sikkim, ***Haryana***, ***Maharashtra***, Puducherry, Uttarakhand
Third Quartile (91,846-1,20,683)	***Gujarat,*** Kerala, Tamil Nadu, Karnataka, Himachal Pradesh, Telengana, ***Punjab***, Andaman and Nicobar Is.
Second Quartile (58,166-91,845)	Mizoram, Andhra Pradesh, Arunachal Pradesh, **Rajasthan,** Tripura, **Chhattisgarh,** Nagaland, Jammu and Kashmir
First quartile (Less than 58,165)	**Odisha,** West Bengal, Meghalaya, Assam, **Madhya Pradesh**, Manipur, **Jharkhand, Uttar Pradesh, Bihar**

Source: Authors' calculations from data provided by Central Statistics Office, Ministry of Statistics and Programme Implementation, Government of India.

So what seems to work in reducing malnutrition among children and women during the thousand-day period in the lower income states vis-à-vis the higher income states? To answer this question, I select four States, namely Bihar, Chhattisgarh, Gujarat and Haryana, with varying levels of economic prosperity and nutritional outcome (Table-3.3) and explore the various proximate determinants that influence nutritional outcomes during the 1000 day period.

Among the selected states, Bihar is the poorest with only about three percent of the people belonging to highest wealth quintile and Haryana is the richest with about 47 percent of people belonging to highest wealth quintile. Chhattisgarh lies below national average in this aspect. Bihar and Chhattisgarh also appear to have lower percentage of women with secondary education which is interesting given the fact that both these states have performed well in terms of reducing specific malnutrition conditions (prevalence of stunting and anemia in Chhattisgarh and that of wasting and anemia in Bihar). All the states, except Bihar, have nearly four in five employed women being paid in cash. The child sex ratio is much lower than the national average in both the developed states. It is also quite

Table-3.3: Economic Prosperity and Malnutrition: Scenario in Selected States

	Category	*Per Capita SDP*	*Ranking in terms of Anthropometric Parameters*	*Summary of observations*
Bihar	EAG	Rs. 23,987/-	Child malnutrition: Stunting-1 (23), Wasting-10 (4), Underweight – 2 (6), **Anemia**- 4 (8) Women malnutrition: Severe underweight 3(10), Overweight or obese- 29 (*21*), Anaemia- 4 (10)	□ Over-all poor conditions of nutrition; □ Stunting is a major problem with very little decadal change □ Prevalence of wasting and anemia also very high but considerable improvement
Chattisgarh	EAG	Rs. 63,791/-	Child malnutrition: Stunting-8 (1), Wasting- 6 (*22*), Underweight – 6 (9), Anemia- 25 (2) Women malnutrition: Severe underweight 10(2), Overweight or obese- 28(*23*), Anemia- 19 (*5*)	□ Maximum improvement in reducing stunting □ Wasting is a major problem, with high incidence and decadal increase □ Lower percentage of children and women affected by anemia, and also considerable decadal decrease
Gujarat	Non EAG	Rs. 1,20,683/-	Child malnutrition: Stunting-7 (3), Wasting- 2 (*26*), Underweight – 5 (21), Anemia- 6 (17) Women malnutrition: Severe underweight 1(15), Overweight or obese- 12(*20*), Anemia- 9 (20)	□ Wasting and underweight among children are major areas of concern with high incidence and very little decadal percentage change □ Anemia among both children and reproductive age women also reflect similar scenario as wasting and underweight.
Haryana	Non EAG	Rs. 1,33,591/-	Child malnutrition: Stunting-13 (7), Wasting- 9 (*17*), Underweight – 14 (8), Anemia- 1 (25) Women malnutrition: Severe underweight 19 (5), Overweight or obese- 16(*29*), Anemia- 2 (*24*)	□ Wasting is a major problem with very less decadal percentage change □ Anemia among children and reproductive age women is a serious problem with minimal decadal percentage change

Figures in parentheses indicate ranking in terms of decadal change (Source: Author's compilation from NFHS data) interesting to note that the incidence of marriage among women before age of 18 years is slightly higher in Gujarat (higher than national average as well, one in four women below 18 years is married) compared to Chhattisgarh and that of early child bearing is higher in both Haryana and Gujarat compared to Chhattisgarh. Bihar fares poorly in both these indicators and is placed much higher than India average. Thus it is evident from Table-3.4 that notwithstanding the high incidence, Chhattisgarh (as well as Bihar in terms of reducing wasting and anaemia) have been able to experience positive nutritional outcomes (decadal change) despite lower education level and comparable proportions of cash earning among employed women. This is counterproductive to the essentialist argument that mother's education and cash earning tend to have positive impact on nutrition.

Table-3.4: Background Socio-Economic Characteristics: The Basic Context

Indicators	*India*	*Bihar*	*Chhattisgarh*	*Gujarat*	*Haryana*
Percentage of population in the highest wealth quintile	20	3.3	14.3	29.4	47.1
Percentage of women with 10 or more years of completed schooling	23.3	13.1	17.3	22.3	29.9
15-49 percentage of women with 10 or more years of completed schooling	35.7	22.8	26.6	33.0	45.9
Percentage of 15-49 currently married women who were employed and earning cash	80.0	61.7	81.9	79.5	80.5
Women age 20-24 years married before age 18 years	17.5	42.5	21.3	24.9	19.4
Percentage of women age 15-19 who have begun child bearing (have had a live birth	7.9	12.2	4.8	6.5	5.8
or are pregnant with first child) Child sex ratio	916	935	969	890	834

Source: NFHS-4.

One of the most immediate set of factors that influence good nutritional outcomes is to initiate positive infant and young child feeding (IYCF) practices. Selected parameters of IYCF are presented in Table-3.5. The median duration of breastfeeding is more or less similar in all the four states, and slightly above national average. In

Gujarat, nearly half of the 6-23 months, children have undergone early initiation of breastfeeding followed by Chhattisgarh and

Haryana (all three states above national average). Only one among ten 6-23 months children received acceptable diet in India. However, it is quite interesting to observe that the percentage of 6-23 months children fed a minimum acceptable diet is double in Chhattisgarh compared to Gujarat, Bihar and Haryana also have higher percentages than Gujarat, the latter being much below national average. Consumption of food rich in Vitamin A among 6-23 months children is also the highest in Chhattisgarh, and Bihar lies above Haryana. With respect to consumption of food rich in iron among 6-23 months children, all the States lie below national average, Bihar and Chhattisgarh report equal proportions and both these States report more than two times higher proportion compared to Gujarat. Thus, table-3.5 indicates that over-all quality of dietary intake plays a very important role in nutritional status and both Chhattisgarh and Bihar (in case of minimum acceptable diet and iron rich food consumption) have performed fairly well compared to the two developed states.

Table-3.5: Infant and Young Child Feeding Practices: The Immediate Causes

Indicators	*India*	*Bihar*	*Chhattisgarh*	*Gujarat*	*Haryana*
Median duration of predominant breastfeeding (months) among last-born children born in the three years preceding the survey Percentage of children born in last	5.8 41.5	6.7 35.3	6.6 47.4	6.5 49.7	6.0 42.3
2 years who were breastfed within one hour of birth Percentage of youngest children age 6-23 months living with their mother who are fed a minimum acceptable diet	9.6	7.5	10.9	5.2	7.5
Among the youngest children age 6-23 months living with their mother, percentage who consumed foods rich in vitamin A in past 24 hours	44.1	39.2	62.7	43.8	36.7
Among the youngest children age 6-23 months living with their mother, percentage who consumed foods rich in iron in past 24 hours	17.9	13.8	13.7	5.1	8.0

Source: NFHS-4.

The Government of India launched a plethora of services to provide health care for mother and children. For the purpose of the present paper, these services have been grouped under nutrition specific and broader health care related categories, besides the utilization of the nutrition and food related services provided by the Integrated Child Development Scheme (ICDS) has also been looked into (Table-3.6). It is noted that in terms of the ICDS services, the maximum utilization has been reported by Chhattisgarh. Gujarat shows a lot of scope for improving the utilization of services with percentages hovering around 50 in most indicators, except that of receiving counselling from AWC after child was weighed. It is also noteworthy that the percentage utilizing various ICDS services in Bihar, the poorest state selected is similar to or even higher to those of Haryana, the richest state selected, except with respect to receiving health check-up by children under 6 years of age and receiving counselling from AWC after child was weighed.

Table-3.6: Utilization of Public Services

Indicators	*India*	*Bihar*	*Chhattisgarh*	*Gujarat*	*Haryana*
ICDS services (food and nutrition related)					
Percentage of children under 6 years of age whose received food supplements from ICDS	48.1	34.3	71.7	56.5	37.7
Percentage of children under 6 years of age whose received immunizations	39.8	41.1	62.5	51.2	39.0
Percentage of children under 6 years of age whose received health check-ups	39.7	23.5	67.9	54.2	36.8
Among the children under six years of age, percentage whose mothers received supplementary food from AWCs during pregnancy	51.4	33.2	87.8	55	32.4
Among the children under six years of age, percentage whose mothers received Supplementary food from AWCs during breastfeeding	47.5	32.8	86.8	48.7	29.3
Percentage of children under 6 years of age whose mothers received counselling from an AWC after child was weighed	64.1	50.0	72.9	71.2	68.1
Mother and Child healthcare related					
Micronutrient Supplements					
Percentage of 15-49 years women who took IFA for at least 100 days	30.3	9.7	30.3	36.8	32.5
Percentage of children 6-23 months who were given vitamin A supplements in the six months preceding the survey	59.5 *(17.5)*	60.7 *(23.5)*	69.2 *(26.6)*	70.3 *(14.6)*	66.0 *(26.1)*
Percentage of children 6-23 months who were given iron supplements in the six months preceding the survey	26.1	21.9	35.7	32.0	40.7
Health-care related					
Institutional deliveries	78.9	63.8	70.2	88.5	80.4
Percentage of 15-49 who had four or more ANC visits	51.2	14.4	59.1	70.5	45.1
Percentage of children who received postnatal care from a skilled provider in the first two days of birth	24.2	10.8	34.2	15.7	21.4
% of mothers who received financial assistance under JSY for births	36.4	53.9	66.2	8.9	13.5
% of registered pregnancies for which mother received Mother and Child Protection Card	89.3	79.9	91.4	89.0	92.0
Percentage of children age 12-23 months who received all basic vaccines (BCG, measles, and three doses each of DPT and polio vaccine (excluding polio vaccine given at birth)	62.0	61.7	76.4	50.4	62.2

(Contd...)

Percentage of youngest children age 6-23 months living with their mother who received deworming medication in the six months preceding the survey	31.4	25.0	39.7	28.2	35.0
Percentage of women age 15-49 who had any contact with a health worker (auxiliary nurse midwife (ANM), lady health visitor (LHV), AWW, Accredited Social Health Activist (ASHA), multipurpose worker (MPW), or other community health worker) in the past three months	23.9	23.1	33.2	27.6	29.0

Source: NFHS-4 (Italicized figures in parentheses indicate micronutrient deficiencies as reported in CNNS 2019 Reports)

The percentage of women taking IFA for at least 100 days is higher in both the developed states and is deplorably low in Bihar. About 70 percent of children 6-23 months in Chhattisgarh and Gujarat were given vitamin A supplements in the six months preceding the survey. It is interesting to note that despite comparable percentages of children suffering from Vitamin A deficiency in Chhattisgarh and Haryana, the percentage receiving supplements is higher in the former state than the latter state. Percentage of children 6-23 months who were given iron supplements is the lowest in Bihar followed by Gujarat. Percentage of institutional deliveries is the highest in Gujarat and the lowest in Bihar. While one in two women in India had four or more ANC visits, in Bihar the percentage is as low as 14 and in Gujarat it is 71, Chhattisgarh (59 percent) is higher than Haryana (45 percent). Percentage of children who received postnatal care from a skilled provider in the first two days of birth in Chhattisgarh (34 percent is double than that of Gujarat (16 percent), in Bihar it is remarkably low (only 11 percent). Both the developed states have conspicuously low share of mothers who received financial assistance under JSY for births. Only 50 percent of the children age 12-23 months received all basic vaccines in Gujarat, which is quite alarming, in Chhattisgarh the percentage is 76 and in Bihar and Haryana, the percentage is about 62. With respect to deworming medication also, Chhattisgarh is much higher than Gujarat and Haryana. Evidently, the utilization of health and nutrition related services including those provided by ICDS and JSY appear to be better in Chhattisgarh (and Bihar with respect to only ICDS) compared to the higher income states.

The results discussed so far might evoke the question as to what could have worked towards driving the states, particularly Chhattisgarh, with lower per capita income and education levels towards adopting positive nutrition practices such as adequate dietary intakes, micronutrient supplementations, better utilization of nutrition and health related public services- practices which appear to be eluding the states with higher per capita income and education levels. Gujarat has a dedicated nutrition policy which none of the other States discussed here have. There is no simple answer to this question as positive nutritional outcomes are also a function of broader environmental and institutional factors. Yet, one cannot ignore the importance of information and education in bringing about positive behaviour changes in this context, particularly if we recall the experience of Bangladesh and Nepal as discussed earlier. It is apparent that Bihar occupies the lowest position among the four States with respect to dissemination of nutrition related counselling and education. However, it is worth noting that in Chhattisgarh, the percentages of mothers/fathers who received any nutrition related counselling or education are the highest and nearly twice as much in Gujarat and thrice as much in Haryana with respect to health and nutrition education from AWCs during pregnancy and breastfeeding. Regarding providing counselling for fathers regarding importance of breastfeeding also, the percentages is the lowest in Gujarat followed by Bihar. Thus, it can be observed that counselling regarding the importance of breastfeeding as well as nutrition and healthcare for the mothers still needs to be scaled-up in all these states, except Bihar.

Table-3.7: Nutrition Information/Education/Communication

Indicators	*India*	*Bihar*	*Chhattisgarh*	*Gujarat*	*Haryana*
Among the children under six years of age, percentage whose mothers received health and nutrition education from AWCs during pregnancy	38.5	18.4	78.4	47	28.3
Among the children under six years of age, percentage whose mothers received health and nutrition education from AWCs while breastfeeding	35.0	16.4	73.0	41.6	25.8
Percentage of fathers who said that at some time during the pregnancy, a health provider or worker spoke to them about the importance of delivering in a health facility	64	44.7	77.3	74.2	64.6
Percentage of fathers who said that at some time during the pregnancy, a health provider or worker spoke to them about the importance of proper nutrition of mother during pregnancy	70.3	53.5	81.2	79.2	73.2
Percentage of fathers who said that at some time during the pregnancy, a health provider or worker spoke to them about family planning or delaying next child	58.3	41.6	71.5	68.4	64.4

(*Contd...*)

Percentage of fathers (whose youngest living child age 0-35 months was not delivered in a health facility) who said that during the pregnancy, someone explained to them the importance of breastfeeding the baby immediately after birth	43.4	42.0	64.3	40.8	51.4

Source: NFHS-4.

Summing Up: Implications for Policy

India not only occupies the bottom position among the South Asian countries in terms of malnutrition, but there are large inter-State differences. Although incidences of all the parameters of malnutrition is quite high in India, it is worth noting that incidence of overweight and obesity is increasing with the developed States being located in a higher risk scenario. Although most of the malnutrition burden in India is usually looked upon as an outcome of the poor performances of the EAG states with lower per capita income, the present paper clearly indicates that, notwithstanding the higher prevalence of different malnutrition indicators in these states, their performance in reducing incidences of stunting, wasting and anemia have been remarkable. Now, what seems to have fuelled these positive changes in these poorer states, particularly Chhattisgarh, which even the most developed States have not been able to achieve? The preceding analysis indicates that positive IYCF practices, better utilization of health and nutrition related services including those provided by the ICDS and JSY etc., nutrition counselling appear to have worked for the remarkable performance of Chhattisgarh. These are also the areas where Gujarat and Haryana need scaled up interventions. Bihar has a long way to go to achieve positive achievements in almost all the indicators, yet it has been successful in making some strides towards addressing malnutrition during the 1000-day period. Over-all, more intersectoral interventions are required to scale–up the measures for tackling the menacing burden of nutrition in India; and concerted efforts must be made in this direction, mere higher per capita income or higher State Domestic Products are not going to translate into lower malnutrition burdens.

References

- Black RE, Victora CG, Walker SP, et al, and the Maternal and Child Nutrition Study Group. (2013). Maternal and Child Undernutrition and Overweight in Low Income and Middle-Income Countries. *The Lancet,* 382(9890):427-451. doi: 10.1016/S0140-6736(13)60937-X.

- Horton, R. and Selina Lo. (2013). Nutrition: A Quintessential Sustainable Development Goal. *The Lancet*, 382(9890):371-372. doi: 10.1016/S0140-6736(13)61100-9.
- *Global Nutrition Report 2018*, Retrieved from https://globalnutritionreport. org/ reports/global-nutrition-report-2018/ on 31 October, 2019.
- Government of Nepal. (2012). *Multi-sector Nutrition Plan For Accelerating the* Reduction of Maternal and Child Under-nutrition in Nepal 2013-2017 (2023). Retrieved from https://scalingupnutrition.org/wp-content/ uploads/2013/03/ Nepal_MSNP_2013-2017.pdf on November 5, 2019.
- Ministry of Health and Family Welfare. (2016-2018). *Comprehensive National Nutrition Survey, National Health Mission*, Ministry of Health And Family Welfare, Government Of India. Retrieved from https://nhm.gov.in/
- UNICEF. (2013). *Capacity Building to Strengthen Local Government And Community Participation In Multi Sectoral Nutrition Programmes in Nepal*. Retrieved from http://archive.wphna.org/wp-content/uploads/2013/10/ multisectoral-nutrition-programs-NEPAL.pdf on November 6,2019.
- USAID. (2015). *USAID Office of Food for Peace Food Security Country Framework For Bangladesh FY 2015–2019.*Retrieved from https://www. usaid.gov/sites/default/files/documents/1866/Bangladesh%20_FSCF_ FINAL.pdf on November 3, 2019.
- World Health Organisation, UNICEF, USAID. (2015). *Improving Nutrition* Outcomes With Better Water, Sanitation And Hygiene: Practical Solutions *For Policies And Programmes.* Retrieved from https://apps.who. int/iris/bitstream/ handle/10665/193991/9789241565103_eng.pdf; jsessionid=8D36905C4B724301D0C019D76F21FA88?sequence=1 on 6 November, 2019.
- Improving nutrition outcomes with better water, sanitation and hygiene: practical solutions for policies and programmes, (excerpted from https://apps.who.int/ iris/bitstream/handle/10665/193991/9789241565103_e ng.pdf on 12-04-2019).

4

Common Psychological Problems among Indian Women: Glimpses from Cases as dealt by Mental Health Professional in Private Psychiatry Setting

—Dr. Kannappa Shetty and
Mrs. Prerna Srivastava

WHO defines Mental Health as - "A state of wellbeing in which every individual realizes his or her own potential, can cope with the normal stressors of life, can work productively and fruitfully, and is able to make a contribution to her or his community (WHO, 2018). WHO has laid down a fact file according to which around 20% of the world population suffers from some sort of mental disorder, making neuropsychiatric disorders one of the leading cause of disability in young people (WHO, 2018). Another leading cause of disability is substance abuse. It also reports the suicide rate of 8 lakhs per year with around 75% of the victims belonging to low and middle-income countries (WHO, 2016). Mental health can also act as a mediator to cause many physiological lifestyle diseases such as cardiovascular diseases, diabetes, hypertension etc. There are multiple factors which govern the occurrence of these disorders. These factors can be biological, environmental as well as psychological. It is usually an amalgamation of these factors which together gives rise to a mental disorder. Biological factors usually comprise of genetics, physical illness, injury, abnormality in brain, infections, prenatal damage, lack of nutrition, developmental issues etc. psychological factors include socioeconomic and occupational stressors as well as trauma experienced throughout life. Environmental factors consist of parental style of upbringing, the environment in which one grows up, the environment in which one survives etc.

We are going to discuss some major psychiatric illness such as depression, anxiety, substance abuse, schizophrenia, postpartum depression and psychosis, obsessive compulsive disorder, dissociative disorder, somatoform disorder and eating disorder among women.

Causes for Psychological Problems among women

A woman undergoes an array of hormonal changes starting from menstruation, pregnancy and menopause. These lifetime events in the life of a woman make their susceptibility different than that of males. Starting from the natal period to the old age females are susceptible to different forms of mental disorders. Studies have shown female offspring of females suffering from depression are prone to be more fearful as compared to the male offspring (Grey et.al, 2013). Girls are more prone to pre-puberty anxiety as compared to boys. Girls are prone to depression during the start of their ovarian cycle according to a longitudinal study (Angold, Costello, & Worthman, 1998). During the menstruation, female body undergoes significant changes both physiologically and hormonally. This causes a spectrum of symptoms ranging from mild discomfort to severe unbearable pain, nausea, fatigue etc. Females suffering from severe form are said to have Premenstrual Dysphoric Disorder (PMDD). It is distressing both psychologically and physically. The activity of hormones increases manifolds during the pregnancy. These changes along with physical changes and psychosocial stressors make a woman more susceptible to mental disorders. Postpartum depression is fairly common however it is found to be linked with chronic onset of depression in many of the cases (Wisner et al., 2013). Psychotic and manic symptoms are seen very commonly in the 1st week of postpartum (Munk et al, 2006). Obsessive compulsive disorder is also found to be prevalent as comorbidity during this phase, especially during postpartum depression. Once a woman reaches menopause, the risk of depression also increases. However, the risk comes down significantly post menopause stage (Altemus, 2017).

Depression among women

Case Vignette: A 30 years old lady was brought to the hospital after she attempted suicide. She reported feeling sad and upset most of the days in the last few months. She had lost interest in doing her chores and had stopped going to work as well. She behaved aloof with family members and had cut all contacts from her friends all of a sudden. This was alarming because she was a very outgoing person and loved interacting with people. The family dismissed this change in her behaviour as work stress. It was only when she attempted suicide did the family pay heed to her symptoms. She tried to justify her attempt saying that her life was worthless and meaningless and she would be better off dead than suffer in this horrible life of hers.

ICD-10(1996) describes depression as low mood, loss of interest, increased tiredness, reduced self-worth and self-esteem, ideas of guilt. Worthlessness, suicidal wishes and ideations, disturbed sleep and decreased sleep. It is classified into mild, moderate and severe type, along with presence or absence of psychotic and somatic symptoms. It is also classified on the basis of frequency of occurrence of the episodes with consecutive multiple episodes being termed as recurrent depressive disorder and those episodes occurring intermittently with manic episodes being termed as bipolar disorder. Premenstrual dysphoric disorder is also classified as a type of depression which enlists symptoms caused due to premenstrual changes in the body. Although Depression is fairly common in male population as well, but the hormones and societal pressure makes women 50% more vulnerable to it (Bohra et al., 2015). Domestic violence, sexual assault, marital rape, workplace harassment, abusive relationship, oppression by family members and other psychosocial stressors makes the women in India more prone to depression. In fact, WHO reports (2018) that Indians are amongst the most depressed populations. Lifestyle diseases such as obesity, diabetes, polycystic ovary syndrome also leads to depression in women. Psychotherapy and pharmacological treatment seems to work will with depression patients, however because of biological differences women are advised to be started on lower dose of antidepressants first owing to higher chances of side effects. Comorbidity such as anxiety and eating disorder is also found to be higher in females (Bohra et al., 2015).

Anxiety disorder

Case Vignette: A 25 years old lady was brought to hospital as she refused to go out of her room. She had locked herself up in her room since last one month and refused to come out and interact. The family reported that she was always an introvert person. She was a reserved kid during her childhood and avoided going to any social gatherings. She didn't have any friends during her schooling and college years. She refused to go to other state for higher studies in spite of getting an opportunity to study in a top-notch college. She refused to join any coaching as she found it to be too crowded and suffocating. She would often bunk classes and would often fall short in attendance. She avoided taking bus or any form of public transport and avoided going out alone, as a result of which one family member had to accompany her always. Her symptoms had precipitated last month when she had an unpleasant experience in her work place where she was asked to make a presentation which didn't go well and she had to face humiliation from her team members and seniors. A diagnosis of social anxiety disorder was made and she was treated for the same.

Anxiety is a complex human emotion which arises when the person perceives some kind of danger. It manifests in the form of cognitive, affective and behavioral changes. DSM-IV (1994) classifies anxiety into following categories- Panic disorder (with or without agoraphobia), agoraphobia without panic, social phobia (social anxiety disorder), specific phobia, generalized anxiety disorder (GAD), acute stress disorder, posttraumatic stress disorder, obsessive compulsive disorder, and anxiety disorder not otherwise specified. It has been reported that females shows higher rate of prevalence of the anxiety disorders such as general anxiety disorderand phobia (Reddy & Chandrasekhar, 1998). In pediatric population, the occurrence of anxiety disorders was found to be at the male to female ratio of 1:2(Trivedi & Gupta, 2010). A study on hysteria showed that its occurrence is significantly higher in case of females. Also, the occurrence was more in unmarried males and married females (Trivedi & Gupta, 2010).

Substance used disorder

Case Vignette: A 35 years old lady was brought to hospital by her husband. She was binge drinking since last few years as a result of which she was facing multiple health issues. Husband reported that she tried quitting multiple times but failed. She was fired from her job last year because of her inefficiency at work, which was again as a result of her drinking. She would drink throughout the days for most of the days. She had stopped noticing her husband and kids completely. She would get abusive towards her husband if he tried to interfere with her drinking habits. The kids were sent to their grandparents to avoid toxic environment at home. The lady refused to seek treatment and tried absconding multiple times from the hospital. She was diagnosed with alcohol dependence and abuse disorder and was sent to rehabilitation centre for recovery.

Substance abuse amongst women in India is an overlooked topic. Substance abuse accounts from overuse and addiction of alcohol, tobacco, cannabis and heroin etc leading to physical as well as mental deterioration. A study conducted on 6000 Indian women indicated heavy use of alcohol, cannabis, opioid and solvents amongst them (Lal, Deb, & Kedia, 2015). The reason behind substance abuse can be attributed to many factors. Certain communities in India encourage consumption of alcohol and tobacco in India. Women of lower socio-economic status are also more open to bidi, betel leaves, country liquor, tobacco etc. Metropolitan cities are also witnessing gradual rise in female substance abusers. A research study showed that females are more susceptible to relapse owing to their reward pathway system (Sinha et al., 2007). Studies claim psychological factors such as sexual abuse, low self-esteem and other psycho-social stressors to be one of the leading causes of substance abuse in females (Brown, Madden, Palenchar, & Cooper-Patrick, 2000 & Dale et al., 2001). Stigmas of the society and poor social support act as hindrances for Indian women to seek help even when they realize the need of rehabilitation.

Schizophrenia

Case Vignette: A 45 years old married lady from rural Karnataka was brought to hospital by her parents. She reported hearing multiple voices since last one year. The voices were that of her dead relatives. The voices would ask her to harm herself and sometimes harm other people as well. The voices would constantly tell her that she is worthless and she should follow what they say in order to be happy. The voices used to command her day to day activity. Because of her psychotic activities her husband an in laws had dropped her to her parent's house and refused to take her back. This further added on to her symptoms. She was diagnosed with schizophrenia.

Schizophrenia is a complex disorder with broad spectrum of symptoms which are characterized into 3 categories namely positive, negative and cognitive. Positive symptoms are those symptoms which are behavior which are not seen in healthy people. Such symptoms include hallucinations, delusions, thought and movement disorders. Negative symptoms indicate lack of normal functionality in psychosocial and occupational aspects. Such symptoms include reduced speaking, inability to feel emotions, less or no expressions of feelings and difficulty in carrying out day to day activities. Cognitive symptoms include loss of cognitive functions such as attention, memory and executive functioning. The prevalence of schizophrenia is almost same in both the genders however the age of onset, symptoms and frequency of symptoms might vary to some extent (Sartorius et al., 1986). The age of onset is later in females as compared to male. Also, the prognosis of the disorder is better in females (Thara & Kamath, 2015).

Mood disorder

Case Vignette: A 30 years old lady was brought to hospital by her husband. She appeared to be extremely talkative. She talked extensively about her achievements and her capabilities. She also reported being in touch with God and asked the doctors to consider her next to God as well. She claimed of making people suffer because of her curse. She also claimed to predict future and offered remedies for all sorts of problems. The husband reported that previous year she was very depressed and was suicidal. She was treated for a depressive episode for the same. After the current episode she was diagnosed with Bipolar disorder, currently in mania.

Mood disorders are also termed as affective disorder. They consist of extreme fluctuations of mood and complications arising from such fluctuations. Bipolar disorder is a very common mood disorder. Bipolar disorder is characterized by occurrence of depression and mania at different time points in a patient's life. They are majorly of two types. Bipolar I is occurrence of full blown mania with intermittent occurrence of depressive episodes. Bipolar II is occurrence of depressive episodes with intermittent hypomania episodes. Cyclothymia is also a type of bipolar disorder which is characterized by occurrence of hypomania and depressive episodes in a duration of 2 years (NIMH, 2018). Although it occurs for both gender but it can be differentiated in case of women by late onset and higher rate of mixed episodes. Also comorbidity such as thyroid, obesity and anxiety are higher in women (Parial, 2015). In case of Indian scenario, bipolar disorder is found to occur mostly in reproductive age of the women owing to various life stressors they face during this period (Chandra, Deepthivarma, Carey, Carey, & Shalinianant, 2003). A study in Los Angles on bipolar patients showed that 60% of bipolar II patients were women. (Hendrick, Altshuler, & Whybrow, 1998) Bipolar symptoms are found to worsen during various menstruation time points as well as postpartum (Rasgon, Bauer, Glenn, Elman, & Whybrow, 2003). Higher chances of relapse of symptoms were found during post partum period (Cohen, Sichel, Robertson, Heckscher, & Rosenbaum, 1995). The diagnosis of bipolar, specially bipolar disorder II should be done carefully for women as it goes misdiagnosed as depression, since occurrence of depressive episodes are more frequent in women (Parial, 2015).

Postpartum disorders

Case Vignette: A 27 year old married lady was brought to hospital by her husband. She had delivered a baby 2 months back. She reported feeling low and incompetent most of the time. She said that she didn't feel any attachment with the baby and hence considers herself to be a bad mother. She was also worried about her career and was afraid that the maternity period will hamper her career growth. She felt lost and worthless. She felt exhausted most of the time and had stopped paying attention to her personal hygiene. She reported passive death wishes as well. She had stopped interacting with her husband and family members as well. She was diagnosed with post-partum depression.

Pregnancy comes out to be a crucial period in a woman's life. She has to undergo multiple physical and hormonal changes which might lead to certain psychological issues. Psychological abnormality triggered post pregnancy is classified into three- postpartum blues, postpartum psychosis and postpartum depression. Postpartum blues are more prevalent and gets resolves on its own within a week. It does not have any major impact on mother's mental health and counseling is sufficient to deal with it. Postpartum psychosis and postpartum depression on the other hand are more serious and often requires hospitalization. 22% of Indian women suffer from postpartum depression (Upadhyay et al., 2017). The symptoms for postpartum depression and postpartum psychosis are same as depression and psychosis respectively.

Obsessive Compulsive disorder (OCD)

Case Vignette: A 35 years old lady was brought to hospital by her family. The family reported that she spent her entire day washing and cleaning the house. The cleaning was so extensive and rigorous that it took most of her time and she was left with no time to carry out any other chores. She also spent around 1.5 to 2 hours every day on her bathing rituals. On being asked she claimed that she didn't feel clean enough in spite of bathing for 2 hours. She also claimed that her house was never clean enough and so she needed to clean it everyday. She would also force her kids and husband to bath several times a day and would get angry if they take less time for the same. She would force them to wash their hands and feet on hourly basis when they are at home. The lady was diagnosed with obsessive compulsive disorder.

Obsessive Compulsive disorder is another psychiatric disorder which seems to affect Indian population; however, the prevalence rate is lesser as compared to European and North American countries. It is characterized as repeated occurrence of thoughts (obsessions) which leads to repeated actions (compulsions). Some of common obsessions are washing, checking and sexual and religious thoughts etc. Gender plays a less significant role in this except that males are found to have early onset as compared to females and they have higher rate of religious obsessions whereas females have higher rate of cleaning compulsions (Reddy, Rao, & Khanna, 2010). Suicidal ideations are one of the high risk behaviour patients of OCD shows. A study on this aspect showed that 59% of the study population had suicidal ideations and 27% had attempted suicide (Kamath, Reddy, & Kandavel, 2007). The patients are linked with severe disability and poor quality of life. The family burden is found to be higher in these patients.

Dissociative disorder

Case Vignette: A 26 years old lady was brought to the hospital. She went missing 5 days ago. She was then found in the neighboring state where she was staying in a hotel. She herself contacted her family. She had no memory of how she reached there. She just claimed that she was returning home from work and then suddenly she found herself in that hotel in the neighbouring state. She did not remember how she travelled, or how she found the place to stay or what she did in those 5 days. The doctors diagnosed her with dissociative disorder.

Dissociative disorder can be understood as loss of connection from one's self and surroundings as a result of major stressful or traumatic events in life. It can be classified into dissociative identity disorder, dissociative amnesia and depersonalization. Dissociative identity disorder was once upon a time known as multiple personality disorder. It is marked my manifestation of two or more personalities with memory gaps ("What Are Dissociative Disorders?," n.d.). Exposure to physical and sexual abuse during childhood makes a person more prone to such disorder. High risk behavior such as suicide and self-harm is found in such patients. A study on Indian population found that the prevalence of this disorder is more in females (Chaturvedi, Desai, & Shaligram, 2010). This might be attributed to multiple stressors Indian women face throughout their lives.

Somatoform disorder

Case Vignette: A 55 years old lady was brought to hospital by her family. She reported having terrible headaches every day and suspected it to be some grave disease. She had consulted multiple doctors across the country and they all couldn't find any causing factor for the pain. All her reports were normal. One of the doctor's had finally referred her to a psychiatrist. On interviewing her in detail, it was found that she was not happy with her family. Her kids were settled abroad and she felt that her husband was not paying any heed to her. She wanted her kids to come back but they refused as they had better career growth abroad. The doctors diagnosed her with somatoform disorder and she was treated for the same.

Somatoform disorder is the term given to disorder in which the patient complains about physical ailment and pain but there is no physiological or pathological explanation behind it. It is basically a way of manifesting stress. Even though the symptoms are psychological, the patient is unaware of it and feels the pain as real. This is in not intentional. It can be associated with personality as well. It leads to social and occupational dysfunction. DSM IV(1994) classifies somatoform disorder into somatization disorder, hypochondriasis, pain disorder, conversion disorder, body dysmorphic disorder, undifferentiated somatoform disorder and not otherwise specified somatoform disorder. They are often found along with depression and anxiety disorder. Women patients are significantly higher as compared to male counterparts (Shidhaye, Mendenhall, Sumathipala, Sumathipala, & Patel, 2013).

Until recent past eating disorder was supposed to be a thing of west, but its prevalence rate is increasing in India currently. It is termed as psychological disturbances leading to abnormal eating habits, such as anorexia nervosa and bulimia nervosa. Anorexia is a term given to the condition of abnormally less eating and starvation in order to maintain low weight. The ideal body weight perception is distorted in such patient. Bulimia refers to a cycle of binge eating and then taking drastic methods to compensate for it so as to maintain ideal weight the perception of which is again distorted. The eating disorders can be life threatening. Several factors lead to this condition some of which are genetic predisposition, personality, cultural beauty standards etc. Studies have indicated that weight concerns amongst Indian students are almost similar to those of their western counterparts (Sharan & Sundar, 2015).

We have discussed some major psychiatric illnesses above. These illnesses cause major psychosocial occupational dysfunction amongst the patients and hence needs to be treated with utmost care. The treatment includes pharmacological interventions as well as psychosocial interventions. Pharmacological interventions refer to drugs which targets the chemical imbalance in the brain which in turn brings down the symptoms of these disorders. Psychosocial interventions are defined as "interpersonal or informational activities, techniques, or strategies that target biological, behavioral, cognitive, emotional, interpersonal, social, or environmental factors with the aim of improving health functioning and well-being". They are administered independently or along with drugs depending upon the severity of the symptoms. They target the symptoms as well as the life post recovery. The patient and the caregivers are taught several strategies to cope up with and manage the disorder.

To conclude, mental health contributes a major chunk to a person's well-being. It has been neglected and considered taboo for a really long time, especially for women. Mental health in India is blooming but still needs to travel a long way. Indian women experience a vast variety of psychosocial stressors owing to their cultural and societal norms. As such awareness of these disorders is mandatory so as to seek help. A team of mental health professionals comprising of Psychiatrist, Clinical Psychologist, Psychiatric Social Worker and Psychiatric nurses are working diligently to provide much needed help and care to mentally ill patients. Their professional guidance along with strong family support is all that a patient needs to lead a healthy normal life.

References

- Altemus, M. (2017). Neuroendocrine Networks and Functionality. *Psychiatric Clinics of North America*, *40(2),* 189–200.
- Angold, A., Costello, E. J., &Worthman, C. M. (1998). Puberty and depression: the roles of age, pubertal status and pubertal timing. *Psychological Medicine*, *28*(1), 51–61.
- Bipolar Disorder, (excerpted from https://www.nimh.nih.gov/health/ topics/ bipolar-disorder/index.shtml on 12-04-2019).
- Bohra, N., Srivastava, S., & Bhatia, M. S. (2015). Depression in women in Indian context. *Indian Journal of Psychiatry*, 57 (Suppl 2).
- Brown, C., Madden, P. A., Palenchar, D. R., & Cooper-Patrick, L.(2000). The association between depressive symptoms and cigarette smoking in an urban primary care sample. *International Journal of Psychiatry in Medicine, 30(1),* 15–26.https://doi.org/10.2190/NY79-CJ0H-VBAY-5M1U.
- Chandra, P. S., Deepthivarma, S., Carey, M. P., Carey, K. B., & Shalinianant, M. P. (2003). A cry from the darkness: women with severe mental illness in India reveal their experiences with sexual coercion. *Psychiatry*, *66*(4), 323–334.
- Chaturvedi, S. K., Desai, G., & Shaligram, D. (2010). Dissociative disorders in apsychiatric institute in India—a selected review and patterns over a decade. *The International Journal of Social Psychiatry*, *56(5)*, 533–539.
- Cohen, L. S., Sichel, D. A., Robertson, L. M., Heckscher, E., & Rosenbaum, J. F. (1995). Postpartum prophylaxis for women with bipolar disorder. *The American Journal of Psychiatry*, *152*(11), 1641–1645. https:// doi.org/10.1176/ ajp.152.11.1641.

- Dale, Glover, Sachs., Schroeder., Offord., Croghan & Hurt(2001). Bupropion for smoking cessationÛ: predictors of successful outcome, *Chest, 119(5)*, 1357–1364.
- Grey, K. R., Davis, E. P., Sandman, C. A., & Glynn, L. M. (2013). Human milk cortisol is associated with infant temperament. *Psychoneuroendocrinology*, *38*(7), 1178–1185. https://doi.org/10.1016/j.psyneuen.2012.11.002.
- Hendrick,V.,Altshuler,L.,&Whybrow,P.(1998).Psychoneuroendocrinology of mood disorders. The hypothalamic-pituitary-thyroid axis. *The Psychiatric Clinics of North America*, *21*(2), 277–292.
- Kamath, P. Reddy, Y. C. J., & Kandavel, T. (2007). Suicidal behavior in obsessive-compulsive disorder. *The Journal of Clinical Psychiatry*, *68(11)*, 1741–1750.
- Lal, Deb & Kedia, (2015). Substance use in women: Current status and future directions. *Indian Journal of Psychiatry, 57(2)*, S275-285.
- Lombardo et al. (2012). Fetal Programming Effects of Testosterone on the Reward System and Behavioral Approach Tendencies in Humans. *Biological Psychiatry, 72(10)*, 839-847.
- Munk-Olsen, T., Laursen, T. M., Pedersen, C. B., Mors, O., & Mortensen, P. B. (2006). New parents and mental disorders: a population-based register study. *JAMA*, *296*(21), 2582–2589. https://doi.org/10.1001/ jama.296.21.2582
- Parial, S. (2015). Bipolar disorder in women. *Indian Journal of Psychiatry*, *57*(Suppl 2), S252–S263.
- Rasgon, N., Bauer, M., Glenn, T., Elman, S., & Whybrow, P. C. (2003). Menstrual cycle related mood changes in women with bipolar disorder. *Bipolar Disorders*, *5*(1), 48–52.
- Reddy, V. M., & Chandrashekar, C. R. (1998). Prevalence of Mental and Behavioural Disorders in India: A Meta-Analysis. *Indian Journal of Psychiatry, 40*, 149-157.
- Reddy,Y.C.J.,Rao,N.P.,&Khanna,S.(2010).AnoverviewofIndianresearchin obsessive compulsive disorder. *Indian Journal of Psychiatry*, 52(Suppl1), S200–S209.
- Sartorius, N., Jablensky, A., Korten, A., Ernberg, G., Anker, M., Cooper, J. E., & Day, R. (1986). Early manifestations and first-contact incidence of schizophrenia in different cultures. A preliminary report on the initial evaluation phase of the WHO Collaborative Study on determinants of outcome of severe mental disorders. *Psychological Medicine*, *16(4)*, 909– 928.
- Seasons and bipolar disorder, (excerpted from https://www.ncbi.nlm.nih. gov/ pubmed/8541932/ on 12-03-2019).
- Sharan, P., & Sundar, A. S. (2015). Eating disorders in women. *Indian Journal of Psychiatry, 57(6)*, 286.
- Shidhaye, R., Mendenhall, E., Sumathipala, K., Sumathipala, A., & Patel, V. (2013). Association of Somatoform Disorders with Anxiety and Depression in Women in Low- and Middle-Income Countries: A Systematic Review. *International Review of Psychiatry*, *25(1)*, 65–76.
- Sinha, R., Fox, H., Hong, K.-I., Sofuoglu, M., Morgan, P. T., & Bergquist, K. T. (2007). Sex steroid hormones, stress response, and drug craving in cocaine-

dependent women: implications for relapse susceptibility. *Experimental and Clinical Psychopharmacology, 15(5),* 445–452.

- Thara, R., & Kamath, S. (2015). Women and schizophrenia. *Indian Journal of Psychiatry*, 57(Suppl 2), S246–S251.
- Trivedi, JK., Gupta, P.K. (2010). An overview of Indian research in Anxiety disorders. *Indian J Psychiatry*, 52, Suppl S3:210-8.
- Upadhyay, R. P., Chowdhury, R., Aslyeh Salehi, Sarkar, K., Singh, S. K., Sinha, B., Kumar, A. (2017). Postpartum depression in India: a systematic review and meta-analysis. *Bulletin of the World Health Organization, 95(10),* 706-717C.
- What Are Dissociative Disorders? (n.d.). (excerpted from https://www.psychiatry.org/patients-families/dissociative-disorders/what-aredissociative- disorders on 12-08-2019).
- WHO (2016). 10 facts on Mental health, (excerpted from http://www. who.int/features/factfiles/mental_health/mental_health_facts/en/ on 12-02-2019).
- WHO (2016). Mental health: Suicide data. (n.d.). (excerpted http://www. who.int/mental_health/prevention/suicide/suicideprevent/en/ on 12-04-2019).
- WHO (2018). Mental health: a state of well-being, (excerpted from http://www.who.int/features/factfiles/mental_health/en/on 18-03-2019).
- Wisner, Sit, McShea, Rizzo, Zoretich, Hughes, Hanusa, B. H. (2013). Onset Timing, Thoughts of Self-harm, and Diagnoses in Postpartum Women With Screen-Positive Depression Findings. *JAMA Psychiatry*, *70*(5), 490–498.
- World Health Organization (1996). *The ICD-10 classification of mental* and behavioral disorders: clinical descriptions and diagnostic *guidelines*. Geneva. World Health Organization.

5

Food-Gender Stereotype: A Sociological Study of Food Preparation in Urban Bengali Household

— *Dr. Nabaruna Mazumdar*

Introduction

Feminists have always been concerned about structured inequalities in society and gender is one such structured inequality in human society. This is because men and women are treated differently in society. They experience different status positions where women are always placed at the bottom of the stratification ladder. Such differential status of men and women are found both within the family and in the public sphere. The concept of gender is derived from the social and cultural meaning attributed to the biological species of male and female. As Kamla Bhasin (2000) stated, gender is a way of differentiating between men and women by assigning them different social roles. The primary role of a woman in human society has been reproduction of children and the responsibility of feeding and caring for the family. On the other hand men have always been responsible for outside household works and is seen as the main bread earner for the household. This difference between regular household chores like cooking, cleaning and caring and that of outside work considerably known as 'paid work' has resulted in differentiating between the status positions of women and men respectively. This is because while domestic work (unpaid labour) is not seen as productive work, outside work is seen as more productive and has high social esteem.

Within the larger area of sociology, anthropology, feminism and culture studies, gender differences and power relations can be best understood through the duality of social roles between men and women. Gender stereotypes about social roles are formed at the time of socialization at a very young age. This grows as cognitive development of the child grows and the child becomes aware of stereotypical gender roles of a man and a woman in society. "Feminists have argued that the family is a major site of inequality where women are subordinated and women's roles perpetuated and also that it institutionalizes heterosexuality- the idea that heterosexuality is both the norm and normal".

On the other hand food is one of the best ways by which gender stereotypes and gender identity gets accentuated. Food plays a major role in constructing gender identity. Earlier food studies refrained from studying the relationship of women and men to food practices. Anthropologists were the first to recognize the importance of food studies and women studies by analyzing food practices. The construction of gender and family through food practices is determined by the fact that food preparation is work that defines family. Studies have shown that feeding practices though an essential part of life is denied as 'work' as it is done by women. For instance decision of planning a meal must be made in a relationship to other people's desires, most importantly husband and then children, and in accordance with what the culture considers a proper meal. Kitchen work is often seen as naturally rewarding for women emotionally as well as aesthetically. Hence domestic food is almost always associated with the wife or the mother.

Objectives of the Study

This chapter explores the relationship between gender and food through preparation, cooking and cuisine within Bengali urban middle class families and the families of the urban poor respectively. The objective is to understand how and why gender roles get constructed, maintained and change across social classes through domestic food habits. This will also reflect on the perpetual gender inequality and gender stereotypes that are prevalent in our society. The paper will also reflect on the comparison of position of women in society among the middle class and the urban poor. The paper will also try to look into the changes that have come about in the stereotypical image of men and women in the private sphere.

While most of food studies concentrate on women and their role in meal preparation, gender faces a backseat. Not much is addressed about men's role in the food processing sector within domestics and outside. However it is much important to recognize the concept of gender while acknowledging food habits and practices of social groups. Food and gender builds on the notion of power and gender division of labour in society along with demarcation of the private and public.

This paper aims to look into the gender power relations and construction of our gender identities through food production, distribution and consumption across the middle class and urban poor households of Kolkata. The paper is a part of a PhD. thesis exploring the food habits of Bengali households among the middle class and urban poor. While the larger study tried to explore the various aspects of social processes through household food habits across social classes, one cannot evade the fact that gender has a major role to play within food practices.

Sociological Perspectives on Food and Gender: A Review

Food can be seen in relation to different aspects of social life but has been a neglected area in the discipline of sociology. Popularized by cultural anthropology, subjects related to food have been taken up by multi-disciplinary perspectives. A research on food and culture cannot miss the works of Mary Douglas (1966, 1971), Anne Murcott (1982), Georg Simmel (1997), Stephen Mennell (1985) and the like. Most of the sociological works on food focus on human diets, social and cultural determinants of diet, changing food patterns of production and involvement of the market, food security at community and household levels etc. Engels's '*Condition of the Working Class in England*' (1969[1845]) has reference of food. In Durkheim's '*The Elementary Forms of Religious Life*' (1912) the concepts of sacred and profane were seen in terms of ritual purity related to food preparation and consumption. It was in the writings of Simmel (1997) that food became a significant point of discourse. Simmel's study on 'meal' perceived the process of eating as an individualized act which is made 'social'.

Murcott (1982) explained that for sociologists food choices are not just dependent on bodily and psychological needs and neither on individual preference but are determined by large number of social factors which makes food habits a good sociological study. For Murcott food habits are shaped by people's relationships and their cultural identity.

There is a dearth of literature on food and gender in Indian society. However some works focus on gender division of labour in the household. Dutta (1999) tried to analyse gender equality and shared gender roles within Bengali middle class families through women's employment status. Dutta (2002) reflects upon the decision making power and authority of working middle class Bengali women. Often the identity of class and gender are merged together. For instance DeVault (1991) addresses issues of class positing that the decision making process to answer question "what's for dinner" is dealt with by working class women through the traditions in their families, and by middle class women by reference to cookbooks and new trends in food preparation. Women are associated with food in terms of not only food intake but also food abstention. Fasting is mostly associated with women and a whole lot of prejudiced, normative rules and regulations which are often linked to religious values and beliefs.

The Method

This paper is based upon an empirical research conducted on Food habits of Bengali households in Kolkata. The study was made on middle class and urban poor respondents respectively. The study employed an ethnographic field research followed by qualitative data analysis. As an exploratory study it focused on the production, consumption and distribution of food within the household of urban middle class and lower class, also the urban poor. By household food it was implied not only cooked foods but all kinds of packaged, processed foods that were bought and consumed. The intention was to look at the different possibilities of food negotiations and reasons that determined respective food choices of the respondents and the other household members.

Household in this case was defined as the group of person living together and taking food from the same kitchen. Often the word 'household' and 'family' have been interchangeably used since almost every household representing the sample were families based on blood or alliance.

The middle class has been identified in terms of white collar professions, salaried and also the self employed people. For the purpose of the study I tried to accommodate different sections of the urban middle class defined on the basis of occupation and education. My respondents mainly belonged to the service class including both public and private sector with minimum education level being school leaving while maximum being a doctorate. I have also included few self employed people with similar educational level. All my middle class respondents live in proper housing in the city and have a distinct cultural life and consumption pattern similar to that believed as the middle class.

I identified my urban poor respondents as those who are employed in the unorganized sector and perform manual labour. They are mostly wage earners working as plumbers, tile *mistry*, bus and private car drivers, domestic helps, ayahs and the like with poor educational level and all of them reside in the slums, lacking proper housing. There are also few self employed people like tea stall owners, vegetable vendors, food vendors.

The study excluded families living below poverty line, people residing in squatter settlements, roadside shelters and street dwellers.

I chose purposive sampling which is a process of non probability sampling technique for my sample. A total of 100 respondents were selected from the middle class among whom 80 percent were women while 60 respondents were selected from the slums among whom 85.5 percent were women. Selection of women respondents were not a conscious process. However it was the women who came forward to act as respondents to discuss on food related matters.

Field study was conducted after visiting the homes of each of the respondents. Data was collected through observation, informal interaction and also semi formal interview. An interview schedule was used in the study. From each family, one person chose to volunteer as a respondent, answering questions on behalf of the whole family. In most cases the respondents chose to answer the questions alone while in some families one or two members of the households too joined in. Interestingly most of the respondents were women. What I found was that the stereotypical view about women and their first hand association with food holds true among the popular belief.

In poor families as well most of the respondents were women. Most of these women work as household maids, cooks or ayahs who returns from work in the afternoon. Taking an afternoon siesta means busying themselves with household chores like cooking, washing, eating or feeding their families. Observation and participant observation were also employed as methods of eliciting information from samples. I could observe their performances while holding conversations and dialogues with the participants. Within the slums, fieldwork enabled me to observe the private spaces of their homes which spoke a lot about their everyday negotiations with food. Some women also shared their problems and asked about remedial measures regarding health problems and alcoholism of their husbands.

The data was analyzed and interpreted in qualitative form keeping in mind the objectives of research. I used the technique of interpretation to analyze my findings. The process of interpretation forms the basis of Weberian sociology which indicates on the 'subjectively intended meaning' that actors relate to their actions. In phenomenological sociology normal everyday life can be interpreted by analyzing the shared meanings among subjects. The phenomenological research and life world helps to analyze the way individuals perceive their own lives or particular phenomena.

Findings: Agents of food preparation

Traditionally women are seen as the prime agents of food preparation and not the men. Domestic food is prepared for the family members who are our near and dear ones. Cooking food for the family is seen as a primary objective of a woman, especially a wife or a mother as it is a process of care giving. Stereotypically women are perceived as the primary care givers of their families. Bengali women are no exception. In other words women are responsible for the proper functioning of the food space or the kitchen which in turn helps to maintain the equilibrium of the household. Over the years Bengali women have been glorified for their aesthetic culinary prowess.

Traditionally women were employed with the skill of producing gourmet delicacies and were even tested for the same by the groom's family during marriage. A woman's life, work and leisure revolved round the kitchen while her sole responsibility was feeding her family. The task of food related activities like, preparation, consumption and distribution of food are highly gendered in middle class and poor households. Women across all social classes are expected to be responsible for the most trivial of household chores, one of which is, providing cooked food to the family.

Food, Gender and the Middle Class

In the middle class Bengali households preparing food is not an egalitarian process which is shared by every family member. Members of the household are usually dependent on one or two female members who shoulder the responsibility of making food for the whole house. While women are seen to perform food related activities inside the home, men are seen to perform other tasks mostly related to outside work. A man's participation in domestic food chores revolve around the purchase of food products from the market which is often performed at the behest of the woman's instructions.

This humble initiative by women shows that the administration of the kitchen is taken up by the women in their own hands and it is her influence that reflects the choice of food purchased for home consumption. Sample data shows that 41percent of the respondents stated that bazaar is bought by the men of the house. It is either the husband or the father in law in most cases who visit the morning bazaar. Some men prefer visiting bazaar in the evening after work. Customarily buying food from the local market have always been a man's prerogative. Like all other public spaces, the bazaar was always a man's social space while women are shrouded within the confines of the kitchen.

The whole act of purchasing food products along with the foods itself is a gendered process. Men are found to purchase more of non vegetarian foods like fish and meat while vegetables, fruits and other grocery products are largely shopped by women. The number of women entering the fresh food bazaar in recent times has increased. Women are in doing more and more of outside household chores that were earlier restricted to men. Women now explore market spaces even without a male escort and shop at their own convenience. A middle aged home maker of south Kolkata states:

> *"I go to the bazaar myself. This is because my husband is not skilled enough to do the bazaar. He being a doctor is always on calls. It is me who takes all responsibilities of the household".*

With changes in the family structure from joint to nuclear and increase in the number of working women per family whereby women share the work space equally with men at home, smaller family sizes, single parent household where often men stay away from home for work, exposure to western culture and global lifestyle, outlook towards this stark demarcation between the public and private are diluted.

Very interestingly non vegetarian foods are again associated with men while vegetarian foods are associated with women. Men are known to cook non vegetarian foods better than women. The perception is in accordance with the idea of women's association with ritual purity. Like non vegetarian foods contain hot substances like onion and garlic in large proportions women in traditional Hindu culture are forbade from consuming it. Such restrictions were there on widows of Bengal for the same purpose. It was assumed that women would lose their sexuality if they ate too much of non vegetarian foods. This notion can be related men's cooking non vegetarian food better than women.

Along with women, Bengali men have also shown keen interest in food preparation. Most of the male respondents claim that they have some exposure to the culinary art in some form or the other. One unmarried thirty years old male said:

> *"My mother cooks regular household meals. We have a maid but we don't give her to cook. I can also cook...I try to make continental food which I am good with...my dad can't cook at all. My mother is the main cook and I am the second cook...I cook only when my mother is not there at home...I can make roti, paratha, luchi better that any girl".*

While men from the lower strata of society cook regular household food in the absence of their women, middle class men mostly engage themselves in leisure cooking. There is a difference between 'duty cooking' and 'recreational cooking'3. Many respondents have reported to perform occasional cooking for leisure in middle class homes. A Christian woman states proudly,

> *"Whenever good food is to be cooked at home, it is my husband who prepares it. I leave the kitchen to him. He is an excellent cook. I make food for my family along with a household attendant and my husband. If there are guests coming home then my husband is the main cook and I become the helper. He has good idea about cooking".*

A middle class husband who works as a researcher talks about the cooking skills of his home maker wife. The respondent is originally from Midnapore district in West Bengal and has his ancestral home in the village. He states:

> *"It is my wife who does the cooking at home. At times I make an omellette for us at dinner. But I know a lot about cooking. Its me who taught my wife how to make food. We don't have any discrimination at home; rather I always help her with food preparation".*

Many of the husbands claimed of teaching their wives the art of cooking in across middle class households. Among the urban educated Bengalis, young girls are often refrain themselves from entering the kitchen or cooking on a regular basis. Girls or unmarried women might take up cooking for recreation or leisure occasionally. In such cases, most women agreed that regular cooking skills have been developed after their marriage in their in laws house.

Cooking and food preparation can also be an empowering job for many. It is through the power to make decisions on what to feed ones family that create hierarchy within the household. On the whole it is easier to ascertain that food choices with regard to cooking rest in the hands of the women be it the mother, daughter, daughter in law in most Bengali middle class households. Few households have reported of sharing the food expenditure among the man and the wife while decisions on food related expenses are collectively administered. However although the choice of food lies in the hands of the woman, the taste preferences of the men and children are always given priority over a woman's choice.

At times women have also reported of preparing meals based on convenience, time, availability of food products and presence of household cooks and not taste preferences of the household members. Ann Oakley (1972), Abbott and Wallace (1997) showed how gender division of labour within families also depend on culture and the family structure. Oakley's (1972) study in Britain revealed how deviant family forms especially among the Asians and Africans organized gender roles in a different way than those of the White Middle Class British families. Similarly in contemporary middle class Bengali households changing lifestyle and culture has brought new changes in gender stereotypes.

Food, Gender and the Urban Poor

Among the lower class, girls from a tender age lay their hands in food preparation along with their mothers and their social roles revolve around the whole act of cooking and serving for the family. Urban poor households often have single women running the house. The woman might be a widow, have estranged husband or an alcoholic husband. Women also have to purchase food products from the bazaars in the absence or indifference of the man of the house. At times women spend their full earning feeding her children and the elderly while the man decides not to contribute to the household food expense. Lower class women on the other hand have dual responsibility of cooking for her family and also earning a living. Most of the respondents from the urban poor households work in middle class homes as domestic helps or cooks. Some are vegetable vendors or help their husband in food stalls. These women lack proper education.

There are certain sections of the lower middle class, especially those working as artisans, petty entrepreneurs or shop keepers who mentioned that decision making power resides with the male members of the household. A woman's identity revolves around the man she is married to. Lack of education, work culture and kind of occupation has been found to influence power relations in the family.

In lower class households it is only the family members who take part in food preparation. In urban poor families women are the primary cooks followed by the elderly women, older children or even at times men. Along with the task of food preparation, shopping for food products are also predominantly undertaken by the women. Nearly 53 percent of the women purchase food for cooking at home in the urban slums while 30 percent of the men go to the market to buy raw vegetables, meat and fish. Lower class women are placed differently in their families compared to their upper class counterparts. While finance is controlled by the men, the hard work is conferred upon the women. 10 percent of the elderly women have reported of purchasing food for home consumption while only 6.7 percent of the children are sent to the market. Elderly women who sit back at home perform small tasks like bringing vegetables from the vendors, chopping vegetables, preparing dal etc in order to contribute to the family chore. On the whole there is greater division of labour among the lower class than the middle class when it comes to food preparation.

In lower class households economic domination is enforced by the men of the house even though their women are working unlike middle class men. While the family budget is controlled by the men, women take up other regular household chores. In such households within the slums, women perform cooking. Around 66 percent of the respondents stated that cooking is performed by the women of the house. While parents leave for work, older children extend their support in domestic cooking. Children often prepare food at home unlike middle class homes.

People from the lower middle class category follow patriarchal norm strictly when it comes to household chores and demarcation is maintained in terms of private and public sphere. Women from such households rely on their men's preference while preparing food. While in middle class households food expenditure is not prioritized over other household expenses, among the lower class food expenditure plays a very important part. Men are in charge of employing decision over how much to spend on food. At times they also state what should be cooked at home on a daily basis. Marxist feminists have perceived economic dependence of women on men as the root cause of their domination and oppression within the household4. These women are mostly dependent on their men folks financially. Even if they are in employment, their wages are insufficient for running the household. At times the elderly matriarchs who take part in food preparation decide on meals and expenses as well. While higher class women especially those who are highly educated and/or working enjoy more autonomy with regard to cooking methods, meals and menus, lower class women are majorly controlled by their men or by the matriarch. Women in such households try to prioritize taste preference and needs of their children and family proudly investing in foods that are consumed by the higher social classes. Among the urban poor, working women however have an upper hand on taking family decisions than non working women. "The choices about who works in the family and who stays at home to care for the household and children are based on the ideology of appropriate gender roles. This is reinforced by labour market factors. The family wage is distributed within the family depending on power relationships between the husband and the wife and who is seen as having the right to decide how and where the money is to be spent"[5].

Changing Stereotypes?

In contemporary times, with more and more women joining work outside home and changes in work culture of men and women, economic changes, changing household structure from joint family to nuclear family and other social and cultural changes, a woman's relationship with the kitchen has undergone subtle changes in many urban middle class homes. Most women in middle class households refrain from cooking on a regular basis. For many of them cooking everyday meals leads to boredom and is seen as a 'treacherous activity'. Young women are particularly not fond of preparing regular household meals. Besides working women are losing dexterity in preparing everyday meal with ease and succumb to external help. This implies that women in contemporary society are devoting less and less time in the kitchen or in food related activities compared to the popular notions. Even homemakers find it futile to spend time in the kitchen. More and more households look for the support of external agents like the household cook or domestic help, who are also women. According to one female respondent:

> *"Cooking depends on my mood. When I have work pressure I don't cook even though my maid is absent"*

An aged middle class home maker confirmed:

> *"When my maid doesn't turn up. I ask for home delivery".*

Middle class women no longer depend solely on home cooked food. Availability of home delivery system by different food joints and restaurants along with small entrepreneurs has also changed women's perception of household food. Different food related mobile *Apps* like *Swiggy* and *Zomato* have made outside food a regular feature of domestic food consumption. Among the younger generation, women resort to recreational cooking more while duty cooking is performed by the elderly members or household cooks. Recreational cooking implies cooking for leisure or recreation. Such cooking is enjoyed by the young independent women who are also economically self-sufficient. For a young media professional:

> *"I love cooking but it is usually different kinds of experimental food that I cook. I never make everyday household meals. We have a cook for that".*

The gradual abstinence of women from regular cooking within the household can be self liberating in a way. Women are no longer compelled to prepare meals at home. They often find other engagements or leisure pass times. This has also made domestic cooks a prized possession. The household cooks have become a dire necessity in middle class homes. The women of the house is usually the one to decide on appointing the cook or domestic help. Keeping a household cook has enormous social significance for the middle class Bengali household. Appointing a cook symbolizes high social status and affluence. In a household with both couples working, a cook is indispensable. In households where women are unemployed and not working cooks are still a necessity.

Nowadays in middle class homes, female domestic helps are preferred as cooks or maids over the males. This was not the scenario earlier when male Brahmin cooks, often *Oriyas* dominated the domestic spaces. These days domestic helps are mostly women. This is yet another instance where women are perceived as natural care givers of society. Women workers also make households feel more secured. This reflects the larger gender discrimination and crime against women that take place in our society. Most middle class households confess of being bothered about the gender of their workers. According to one male respondent:

> *"If I find a male cook then I will be bothered because I am not habituated and will be startled. Besides I will also doubt his conduct inside the house and in my kitchen. May be I will not hire him. As of now no such situation has arisen. Its mostly female cooks that I have got".*

In recent times changes are inevitable with respect to the agents of food preparation and decision making on food choices in the household. While most men and women are working outside home, elderly members both men and women have to take up the responsibility of household management and supervision. In the absence of many senior members in the household of working couples, while cook is hired for making food at fixed hours, cooking is often shared over weekends or holidays. In such cases men show active involvement in food preparation process unlike what it used to be earlier. Wives and mothers who often prioritized cooking traditionally have found other interests in modern times. Women keep themselves busy with other activities outside the home while even older children are encouraged to explore little culinary skills in the kitchen.

> *"My son often fries ready to eat chicken nuggets and eats in the evening whenever he is hungry. He can also make Maggie noodles", claimed a middle class school teacher.*

While cooking food is sourced out to domestic helps or public eateries, decision making process with regard to food preparation and consumption still lie in the hands of the women among the Bengali middle class, where male members seldom interfere. In some families decision regarding what food is to be cooked in the house is a collective affair whereby women approach other household members to know about their preference. According to a middle class homemaker:

> *"I decide on all food matters. I keep in mind the taste and preference of my family members. I try to avoid outside food and cook everything at home".*

Middle class Bengali women take it in their pride to control and manage the hearth. Cooks are delivered detailed instructions as to what and how cooking is to be performed. Unlike the traditional joint families in Kolkata which are dwindling, contemporary nuclear families with both spouses working find a shift in the traditional power structure of the household with special reference to food preparation and decision making. Traditionally it was the family matriarch who presided over the kitchen and food preparation while the lesser women, brides, and daughters succumbed to their authority. Such instances are yet not irrelevant in today's modernized world. One of the respondents who is a newly wed wife stated:

> *"It is mostly my mother in law who decides what is to be cooked. But I decide what to cook when I feel like making some snacks or an added item for dinner or lunch. At times I even cook the whole food when my mother in law is sick and there are people coming over".*

Nonetheless it is not difficult to assert that times are changing. Today middle class households experience greater autonomy, more division of labour and collective decision making with regard to food. In some cases the younger generation men come up with cooking ideas and new cuisines to be tried at leisure. However children's preference and taste are definitely prioritized in smaller nuclear families unlike large joint families. For a thirty nine years old man, cooking on holidays and weekends shared by him and his wife come up with new delicacies to win hearts of their children. Although senior members especially women feature most in this category at times power structure of the household changes which gets exhibited through ones' own right over the kitchen. One of the respondents married for the past twenty years claimed that earlier it was her mother in law who would decide on what food to be cooked and eaten at home.

> *"Foods were more of a traditional kinds like thor and mocha. But now I decide what is to be eaten. We don't have a whole time cook but only a thike who comes and makes lunch. It there is rooti or paratha for*

dinner then the maid cooks before leaving. But of different kinds of cuisine it is I who cook while she only does the jogar. Such foods were never prepared during the time of my mother in law".

With changing times the gender stereotypes within the household of urban middle class are changing. New types of cuisines, fast foods, packaged foods and multi-culinary foods are finding a place on the food platter in large amounts. However cooking and feeding is still largely a woman's domain across social and economic classes. Unlike middle class women, women in lower class Bengali households experience much less autonomy within the household. The food choices for the urban poor are also much limited compared to the middle class.

Conclusion

One cannot evade the question of gender when it comes to food habits especially among Bengali households. Household food habits are associated with issues like domestic labour, power relations, gender roles, class and status. Class difference and unequal access to education, employment and skills create differences in the way women negotiate with their roles and status within the family. The needs, desires and problems of lower class women are very different from the middle class women.

Women have always been the providers of food while the men and other family members are mere recipients. Food choices are largely determined by the women of the house, young and old. Even though male participation within the household is increasing among the middle class and is found among the poor, it is majorly still a woman's domain. Women not only prepare food but also play the task of distributing food among the household members. However gender division of labour within across social classes in terms of food is much limited. Women largely feel controlling the domestic hearth is a space that brings them power.

References

- Abbott, Pamela and Wallace, Claire. 1997. *An Introduction to Sociology: Feminist Perspectives*. London and New York: Routledge.
- Avakian, A.V and Haber, Barbara. 2005. *From Betty Crocker to Feminist Food Studies: Critical Perspectives on Women and Food*. Amherst: University of Massachusetts Press.
- Bhasin, Kamla. 2000. *Understanding Gender*. New Delhi: Kali for Women.
- Carole Counihan and Penny Van Esterik (eds.). 1997, 'The Culinary Triangle', in *Food and Culture: A Reader*. New York, London: Routledge Taylor and Francis Group.

- Deshpande, Satish. 2006. "Mapping the 'Middle': Issues in the Analysis of the Non Poor Classes in India, in Mary E John. (eds). Contested Transformations: Changing Economies and Identities in *Contemporary India*. New Delhi: Tulika Books.
- DeVault, M.L. 1991. *Feeding the Family: The Social Organization of Caring as Gendered Work*. Chicago: University of Chicago Press.
- Douglas, Mary. 1972. Myth, Symbol and Culture. *Journal of American Academy of Arts and Science*. 101(1): 61-68.
- Durkheim, Emile. 1915. *The Elementary Forms of Religious Life, A Study in Religious Sociology*. London, New York: G, Allen and Unwin, MacMillan.
- Dutta, Mousumee. 1999. Gender equality in families: Bengali middle class employed women in India. *Contemporary South Asia*. 8:2, 161-176.
- Dutta, Mousumee. 2002. Women's power and authority within middleclass households in Kolkata. *Contemporary South Asia*. 11:1, 7-18.
- Engels, F. 1942. *The Origin of the Family, Private Property and the State*. New York: International Publishers.
- Engles, F. 1969. *Condition of the working class in England*, Panther Edition, New York and London https://www. marxists.org
- Featherstone, Mike and Frisby, David (eds.). 1997. *Simmel on Culture: Selected Writings*. Sage Publications.
- Mennell, Stephen. 1985. *All Manners of Food: Eating and Taste in England and France from the Middle Ages to the Present*. Oxford, U.K, New York, U.S.A: Basil, Blackwell.
- Murcott, Anne. 1982. The cultural significance of food and eating: *Proceedings of the Nutrition Society*. 41. 203.
- Murcott, Anne. 2000. Understanding Lifestyle and Food Use: Contribution from the social sciences. *British Medical Bulletin*. 56(1): 121-132.

6

Education of Tribal Women in India: A Comparative Analysis

— *Dr. Ruchiraj Upadhyay*
& Ms. Meeraba Jadeja

Introduction

The paper has mainly emphasized on women education in India and especially contemporary status of education level in schedule tribe women. Scholar has analyzed the women education rate and male female gap in literacy rate in various decades since 1951 to 2011. This paper examines the status of Scheduled Tribe women compared to others. The women belonging to schedule tribes are exploited and discriminated. On one hand, they were discriminated on account of their tribal status and on the other; they were discriminated on gender lines. At every place tribal women are exploited and suffer more than others. Tribal women become victims of exploitation far more than Savarna women or the women who belong to other caste groups and categories. As a matter of fact, it has been found that at workplace tribal women labors are also getting exploited physically by owners and officers. This paper also expresses the picture of literacy rate of tribal women in India and impact of status on their education. It has been found that literacy rate in scheduled tribal women is very low even after seven decades of independence and many reasons behind it which has been examined in this paper. In a very true manner, socio-economic backwardness are the main considerations for less education in tribal women. Noteworthy, status of scheduled tribal women in general and in their community are playing important roles for their educational upliftment. Eventually the paper indicates such steps to access the women education in schedule tribes. Thus, this paper comprised the women literacy rates in India, caste and community-wise status of women, role played by Scheduled

Tribe women in general and in their society, and impact of status and role of Scheduled Tribe women on their education.

Today study about the woman education is an emerging topic in contemporary India because after 7 decades of independence, female education ratio is still found to be very low compared to male education ratio. Noteworthy, Indian Hindu society has a patriarchal structure, where there is more importance of male birth than female birth. Male has a superior status than female in every function of Hindu society.

As a matter of fact, the status of women is lower in Indian Hindu society. Conversing about Schedule Caste women, due to poverty and economic crisis status of Scheduled Caste's women is also found to be very low. However, in social system, Dalit women have better status in Dalit society compared to the Savarna women. Out of the caste scenario, tribal communities are also suffering from poverty and economic crises but in tribal women status is better than Hindu savarna women status in social structure. Here, we can say that the status of women is definitely very low in Indian society but if we distinguish it in different manner (socio-economic perspective) we can trace lots of variations between the status of Savarna, Dalit and tribal women. These are the general observation among the social status of women but if we take a glance upon perceptions among women education we can trace the similar situation among all the women belonging to various caste and communities. This article is not comparative analysis between the status of Tribal, Dalit and Savarna women, but it intended to explain about patriarchal Indian society where there were not given importance to women education. Here author has tried to depict the facts among the women education and particularly status of Scheduled Tribe women in Education.

Education

When we talk about educational status we have to grave upon the meaning of Education. Furthermore, when we have to see the proportion of education in particular community we have to take a glance upon the beliefs and awareness among education in that community. Here scholar has defined the Education by different perspectives.

As we can say that Education is a dynamic process, basically it commences from the birth of child according to the pragmatic context. In sociological sense it is a part of socialization process of Individual. In the context of Indian Hindu Culture, according to Vedas, 'Education makes man self-reliant and selfless'. (Rigveda). Noteworthy, most of the traditional philosophers and revivalists of India has explained education in following spiritual way (https://www.preservearticles.com/short-essays/short-essay on- the-meaning-of-education/17999):

"Education is the realization of the self" – Adi Shankracharya

"Education is a divine perfection already existing in man" - Vivekananda

"Education is means for character formation" – Dayanand Saraswati

"All-round drawing out of the best in body, mind, spirit" – Mahatma Gandhi.

Thus we can see that most of the Indian philosophers have shown Education as a mean of self-realization" similarly modern thinkers has also explain its meaning in different way and today in the 21st century we can see the similar definition of education such as it is a process of enrichment and enlightenment of individual. Furthermore, Dr. Zakir Hussain has defined education as a "process of individual mind, getting to its full possible development". Many western (modern and classical) thinkers have also defined the education as under:(https://www.preservearticles.com/short-essays/shortessay- on-the-meaning-of-education/17999).

"Education is the capacity to feel pleasure and pain at the right moment. It develops in the body and in the soul of the pupil all the beauty and all the perfection which he is capable of." – Plato

"Creation of sound mind in the sound body" – Aristotle

"Education is the natural, harmonious and progressive development of man's innate powers." – Pestalozzi

Hence, Western thinkers are also addressed education as 'development of mind, body and soul'. They also emphasize over the education as a capacity builder of individual. Thus, here we can say that either Indian and western thinkers are having similar perceptions among education. Here scholar didn't mean to compare the thoughts and theories of Indian and Modern thinker among education but here he has tried to explain the meaning of education in its straight form. In short, education is a process of empowerment, enrichment and enlightenment.

Scheduled Tribe

Tribals are basically known as Aborigins, origins or moolnivasis of India. As per the constitution, they are known as Scheduled Tribes in India. In other words, these tribal people are known as Girijan, Parijan or Aadivasis.

Socially, economically and culturally they are connected with Jal (Water), Jangal (Forest) and Jamin (Land). Generally tribal people are connected with the old pattern of agriculture. Due to the geographical disparities and less of modern agricultural knowledge they become deprived from the agricultural reformation. Though, their traditional farming pattern and living pattern played an important role to sustain them in the odd situation of forest geography. Their economic life is connected with the raw forest production. Tribal women are playing an important role in the income generation activities i.e. to collect forest products like honey, gum, east Indian ebony, mahuvaane flame of the forest etc. with their other family members. Generally the resident of tribes is at mountain, forest and hilly areas; this is the reason that they are far from the mainstream society physically. However, in contemporary era, due to the transportation and communication means as well as with the constructive efforts of government and non-government organizations tribes are now developing. Increasing rate of education played an important role to upliftment of tribal community in India. Currently as per the census 2011, there are 8.2 percentage tribal people are living in India. Here scholars have emphasized and comparatively analysed the status of women education in tribal community and other communities of India.

Women education in India

Education is a mile stone for the empowerment of women. As Vivekananda said "The best thermometer to the progress of a nation is its treatment of its women" (Swami Vivekanada, 2005). Noteworthy, there were many social reformer and social revivalists i.e. Dayanand Saraswati, Jyotiba Phule, Raja Ram Mohan Roy, Swami Vivekanand, Ani Besant and many others has put their efforts to change the status of women and uplift them. Education makes the women self-dependent and self-esteemed. Indian National policies are also favoring the women empowerment and make them male equivalent. As mentioned in the policy of government for women empowerment (2001), "Equal access to education for women and girls will be ensured. Special measures will be taken to eliminate discrimination, universalize education, eradicate illiteracy, create a gender-sensitive educational system, increase enrolment and retention rates of girls and improve the quality of education to facilitate. Moreover, it contents that, sectoral time targets in existing policies will be achieved, with a special focus on girls and women, particularly those belonging to weaker sections including the Scheduled Castes/Scheduled Tribes/Other Backward Classes/ Minorities" (National Policy for women empowerment, 2001) Thus, women empowerment through education has emphasized in the policies by Government. Along with that many NGOs are efforts to enhance the women education since national freedom.

However, after the six decades of freedom and despite continuous efforts of Government and Non-Government Agencies, women education ratio cannot be found equivalent to male education ratio. It is because of gender discrimination and gender inequality in Indian social system. The status of woman was considered much lower than the man and she has to stay between the four walls of home too in the conservative society. In this sense, stereotypical attitudes, discriminatory behavior, tendency to push marginalizing women and the rejection of male equivalent status by Patriarchal society were the key indicators which became barrier in women education in past. Similarly, its influence is still prevalent in female education in India today. Here it analyzes the literacy rate in different decades.

Decadal Growth of Female literacy rate in India – 1951 to 2011

Sl. No.	*Census Year*	*Person*	*Female*	*Male – Female gap in Literacy*
1.	1951	18.33	8.86	18.30
2.	1961	28.3	15.35	25.05
3.	1971	34.45	21.97	23.98
4.	1981	43.57	29.76	26.62
5.	1991	52.21	39.29	24.84
6.	2001	64.83	53.67	21.59
7.	2011	74.04	65.46	16.68

Source: Census of India 1951 to 2011.

- Literacy rates for 1951, 1961 and 1971 Censuses relate to population aged five years and above.

- The rates for the 1981, 1991, 2001 and 2011 Census relate to the population aged seven years and above

- The 1981 Literacy rates exclude Assam where the 1981 Census could not be conducted. The 1991 Census Literacy rates exclude Jammu & Kashmir.

Data of different decades summarized that the rate of Women education has increased gradually, but during last 2 decades it has been increasing very rapidly by effective policies among women education as well as increasing awareness to its requirement. “However, women’s education got a boost after independence and the new government took effective measures in this regard” (Chauhan, 2011). As a matter of fact, Female education is utmost important for any developing country and in this context 65.46% female literacy rate inadequate. Noteworthy, educated women are playing an important role for social and economic development for a country. Even education in woman is supporting to set up healthy and qualitative family life, promote education in their children, guide them for their better future and makes them a liable citizen of nation. Thus, women education is far favorable to build a progressive nation.

According to Chauhan (2011), "Although in the *Vedic* period women had access to education in India, but they gradually lost this right". During and after the British Rule, many social reformer and revivalists (as mention above) have emphasized for women education through various socio-religious movement in India. However, approach among women education has become positive in Indian society, though these efforts could not immediately influence on women education. It is because of the disappointment of Large conservative class of Indian society among women education at past. Today, in the 21st century this conservative approach has been change in very large extent. It is inherent that if women education ratio has taken 6 decades to increase up to 50 per cent, than it will take time to reach up to 100 percent. Moreover, the people of rural India also seems very disappointing among women education compared to urban India according to the data revealed by census. In 1961, Female Education rate was 11% in rural India compared to 43.75% in Urban India respectively. Subsequently, the rate of female literacy rate in rural areas has gradually increased i.e. 16.86% in 1971, 21.35% in 1981, and 30.17% in 1991. Noteworthy, in 2001 female literacy rate in rural India was 46.12% compared to 72.86% urban areas and in the year 2011 it increased up to 58.75% in rural areas compared to 79.92% in urban areas (Census, 2011). These all data shows that during the decade 1991 to 2001 the ratio has increased very high compared to other decades in Rural India but it could not reach up to the ratio derived by urban areas. It all depends on the approaches of the people of conservative society which could not accept to give education to the women or need to give education to the women of their family. It needs time to change the approaches of the people who are total conservative. Schooling drop out ratio has also seen very high in India compared to many other developing countries. Every female cannot reach up to higher education, which got admission in the school. Migration, fail in examination, far located school from the house and to give importance to marriage than education in conventional families etc are the indicators for high female drop out ratio in India. These all are the reason can recommend for low women education ratio. In short we can say that after the 6 decades of Independence, education ratio remains low in women compare to the men and in rural areas compare to the urban areas (https://phd-photos. blogspot.com/2011/04/womens-education-inindia- has-been-one.html#).

Status of Scheduled Tribe women in India

Status of tribal women could be judged by their role playing in society as well as it depends on the authority which she enjoyed in the community. Male determine authority is called patriarchy and female determine authority is called matriarchy. Various tribal communities follow the patriarchy and matriarchy both kind of authority in India. Moreover, authorities is depends on descents also, weather it is patrilinear or matrilinear. Most of the tribal communities are patrilinear except Khasi, Jaintia, Garo etc and such tribal communities of Meghalaya of North East India who follow matrilinear system. Regarding the status of tribal women is relatively high in their society as this society is characterized like egalitarian societies. There is not any kind of hierarchy like caste system in Indian Hindu society. On an average mostly in Indian families characterized by patriarchal society, male child is getting more privileges compared to female child during their socialization process (abstract but fact in mentalities). But tribal society's female child is treated as equally as male child. Male-female sex discrimination is not raised in tribal social system. Compared to the other castes, the tribals are "educated without education", as they give equal rights to women like men. If we see particularly in literacy rate of Tribal women, tribal women are more illiterate compared to man in their community and even compared to other social groups also. Moreover, because of their illiteracy they suffer a lot in the streamlining societies. A hard working tribal woman is suffering lot at her workplace especially in unorganized sector where there are lots of issues regarding their safety, security as well as wages also.

Noteworthy, Gender roles, rules and regulation constructed by society is always in centre in the mentality of Indian people. The family structure of India believed mostly in patriarchal society and they also follow it except some tribal communities. Patriarchy denotes the power, supremacy and domination of men. So, directly or indirectly the Indian people believe that women are inferior than men. Because of the discrimination of women and of class and caste system, tribal women suffer a lot. The structure of tribal society is totally different from others. We cannot find any kind of dowry system on marriage in Tribal. The widowed or divorced women are free to marry again. The Tribal women also have freedom in the selection of their life partner. If she became pregnant before marriage, then either the boy has to marry the girl or has to pay the compensation to her family. The child is born in her natal family and it does not have an effect on her marriage prospects in any way. So, we can say that, compared to other social groups and communities, the tribal women got more freedom in their life (https://www.researchgate.net/ publication/336936951_ social_ and_heal'th_status_among_sahariya_tribal_women_in_ gwalior_division_ a_situational_analysis).

Tribal women are very strong and courageous in handling of environmental activities. We can say that, the Tribal are too much dedicated to the nature. They adored and worship the natural things, like tress, hills etc. They believe in superstition and rigid rituals of religion which they made. The Tribal women work hard in labour than men. So, they are also very strong in economic income generation activities. Moreover, it is awkward to and time bound fact to change the patriarchal mentality of the society in which, the roots of discrimination and gender bias are stored. Women in tribal communities are none or less suffered compared to other communities and categories.

Khasis, Nagas, Garos, Bhills, Gond, Dubala, Dhondiya, etc. are the tribal communities in India. Women in Garos and Khasitribal communities of north east India are deriving good status in their communities due to their existing Matriarchal social system. The another differences we can see in the tribes like, Ho and Gond the husband does not want to always enjoy a dominant role. So, we can say that the position and status of Tribal women are totally different from other Indian Castes and communities (https://www. researchgate.net/publication/336936951_social_and_heal'th_ status_among_sahariya_tribal_women_in_gwalior_division_a_ situational_ analysis).

Education of Scheduled Tribe women in India

Trend of Education of women in schedule tribe is shown in different forms during various decades. In 1961, literacy rate in India of Schedule tribe's women was on 3.16%, which has increased up to 4.85% in 1971, gradually 8.4% in 1981 and 18.19% in the year 1991. After a decade in the year 2001, women education ratio in tribal women was increased up to 34.76% in India. This is the 16.57% high decadal growth from the year 1991 to 2001. From overall glance, education ratio has increased but it was not adequate to connect and mélange the STs women in the mainstream comparatively. Subsequently if looking among the education ratio in 2011.

The table shows that total literacy rate in India was 49.4% which become little bit increased compared to the last 4 decades. Moreover, Rajasthan, Bihar, Orissa, M.P and States like J&K, are derived very low female literacy rate where as Mizoram, Meghalaya, for female literacy rate which derived more than 60%. There is Manipur, Goa, Tripura Kerala,

State/ UT& Sex wise Literacy Rates of Scheduled Tribes (Census 2011) (Figures in percentage)

Sl. No.	*State/UTs*	*Person*	*Total Male*	*Female*	*Person*	*Rural Male*	*Female*	*Person*	*Urban Male*	*Female*
1.	Andhra Pradesh	49.2	58.3	40.1	46.9	56.1	37.7	66.8	74.7	58.7
2.	Arunachal Pradesh	64.6	71.5	58.0	60.4	67.7	53.3	84.6	90.3	79.4
3.	Assam	72.1	79.0	65.1	70.9	78.0	63.8	90.0	93.7	86.3
4.	Bihar	51.1	61.3	40.4	50.3	60.7	39.5	65.3	72.5	57.6
5.	Chhattisgarh	59.1	69.7	48.8	57.6	68.4	47.1	76.9	84.9	69.0
6.	Goa	79.1	87.2	71.5	78.4	86.4	70.7	80.2	88.3	72.7
7.	Gujarat	62.5	71.7	53.2	61.3	70.7	51.8	72.7	80.0	65.1
8.	Haryana*	-	-	-	-	-	-	-	-	-
9.	Himachal Pradesh	73.6	83.2	64.2	73.0	82.7	63.4	87.4	92.5	81.9
10.	Jammu & Kashmir	50.6	60.6	39.7	49.1	59.3	38.3	71.7	79.6	62.6
11.	Jharkhand	57.1	68.2	46.2	55.2	66.6	43.9	75.4	83.2	67.8
12.	Karnataka	62.1	71.1	53.0	59.0	68.5	49.4	74.8	81.9	67.7
13.	Kerala	75.8	80.8	71.1	74.0	79.3	69.0	90.4	92.7	88.2
14.	Madhya Pradesh	50.6	59.6	41.5	49.3	58.4	40.1	66.7	74.0	59.2
15.	Maharashtra	65.7	74.3	57.0	63.2	72.2	54.1	80.3	86.1	74.1
16.	Manipur	77.4	82.1	72.7	75.9	80.8	71.1	87.7	91.6	83.9
17.	Meghalaya	74.5	75.5	73.5	71.0	72.2	69.8	91.3	92.3	90.3
18.	Mizoram	91.5	93.6	89.5	84.5	88.6	80.2	97.9	98.4	97.5
19.	Nagaland	80.0	83.1	76.9	76.0	79.5	72.4	92.6	94.6	90.6
20.	Orissa	52.2	63.7	41.2	51.1	62.7	39.9	69.1	77.7	60.5
21.	Punjab*	-	-	-	-	-	-	-	-	-
22.	Rajasthan	52.8	67.6	37.3	51.7	66.7	36.1	69.0	81.0	55.6
23.	Sikkim	79.7	85.0	74.3	77.5	83.2	71.4	89.2	92.9	85.6
24.	Tamil Nadu	54.3	61.8	46.8	51.3	59.0	43.6	69.1	75.4	62.7
25.	Tripura	79.1	86.4	71.6	78.4	86.0	70.7	92.2	94.8	89.7
26.	Uttar Pradesh	55.7	67.1	43.7	54.5	66.2	42.3	67.0	74.8	58.0
27.	Uttarakhand	73.9	83.6	63.9	72.4	82.5	62.0	88.3	93.7	82.6
28.	West Bengal	57.9	68.2	47.7	56.7	67.2	46.2	71.2	78.4	64.0
29.	A & N Islands	75.6	80.9	69.9	74.2	79.8	68.2	95.2	98.0	92.6
30.	Chandigarh*	-	-	-	-	-	-	-	-	-
31.	Dadra & Nagar Haveli	61.9	73.6	50.3	58.5	70.8	46.3	79.5	88.0	71.1
32.	Daman & Diu	78.8	86.2	71.2	79.6	87.5	71.7	78.0	85.0	70.7
33.	Delhi*	-	-	-	-	-	-	-	-	-
34.	Lakshadweep	91.7	95.7	87.8	91.5	94.7	88.3	91.8	96.0	87.6
35.	Puducherry*	-	-	-	-	-	-	-	-	-
	India	59.0	68.5	49.4	56.9	66.8	46.9	76.8	83.2	70.3

Source: Census of India, 2011.

and UTs i.e. Daman and Diu and Lakshadweep are the front runner states the highest 89.05% STs Female literacy rate in Mizoram which is appreciable. Thus, we can see the lots of variation among schedule tribe's female literacy rate by different states. Even there are vast differences between the male female literacy rates in schedule tribes. We can see that only 49.9% STs women are include in the definition of literates compare to the 68.5% male categories and this situation has also exhibit in all states of India. Even vast different has revealed between rural and urban scenario in every states . Female are having high literacy rate in urban areas compared to the rural areas in each state. In Daman and Diu female literacy rate in rural areas are little higher than urban areas which depends on their geographical and socio-cultural situation. Moreover, Male are having high literacy rate compared to the female of schedule tribes. Thus we can see the area wise, state wise and gender wise different scenario of educational ratio in India according to census, 2011.

Tribal people are living in forest and hilly areas, the only source of their earning is farming and collecting forest produce. Tribal woman plays very important role in income generation activities. This may be a reason for their less educational ratio. Education is only a thing or we can say 'weapon' to come out of the tribal communities from the poverty and degraded conditions. Tribal communities are always humiliated by other social groups. Tribal women are still suffering a lot through their less educational status. Poverty, gender discrimination, race discrimination etc. are the indicators which exploit tribal women a lot. In that context, increasing ratio of education is an important indicator for tribal women to make them able to live prosperous. Present condition of Tribal women in urban areas especially migrated is very much challenging.

There are many reasons behind less ratio of women education in schedule tribes as mention in the status of women in tribal communities. Most of the women from schedule tribes are belonging to poor families and it is utmost important to do income generating activities to sustain for and with their families. Even approaches among the people of STs are mainly given the importance to their current requirement which shows their compulsion. Firstly, they need to fulfill their basic requirements. As mentioned earlier that in tribal areas most of the women are doing agricultural labor with the male in their families and urban areas they are also working mostly at non-organized sector. Many women have to expand their life for laboring for income generation and in this situation they could not give upon their children education also which is a barrier. Most of them are thinking that if their girl child has to be adopted this same work in future, than better to not teach further. Tribal families are migrated to urban areas finding their income generation activities and mostly got work at unorganized sector, where tribal women lived with lots of struggle with lack of even basic amenities. Sometimes, women get married at their very young age, which stops their schooling. It has been found that due to the unemployed condition girl's parents are forced to work. Mostly, it has found that those who are living in low income settlements, girl child were forced to take care of her siblings when parents went at work. Moreover, unawareness of the importance of women education, influence of streamlining patriarchal society, insecurity, fear of insecurity, distance of educational institutes from their households etc. are mentionable causes for stopping schooling girl child. Furthermore, social disappointment and other traditional values for women education, lack of social recognition and less important to female education, poverty etc. are also the mentionable causes for less women education. Poverty can be considered for less women education rate because many times due to high fees or other expenses families are not allowed to teach girls and even drop-out ratio in school has also shown high because of same reasons. Very few numbers of girls can get education in privatized institutes. Thus, socio-economic backwardness are the main considerations for less women education in schedule tribes.

Steps to access the women education in Scheduled Tribes

Government of India has taken many steps to access the women education in schedule tribes for over 7 decades. Noteworthy, it has not become more effective till the date as data shows earlier. Still the policies and planning are working properly to increase women education in STs. Many educational laws have stimulated the women education. Education is a key indicator for women empowerment and in this context authority of India has introduced some programs like free education for women, scholarship and fellowships for women, National Program for Education of Girls at Elementary Level (2003), Right to Education etc and some other government welfare schemes. Even reservation in Education has also become fruitful to the women especially belonging to the Schedule Tribe women. Though large amount of Tribal women are deprived from primary to higher education. Government of India has been making concerted efforts since independence for bridging the socio-economic gap between the advantaged and the disadvantaged groups, but still these sections have remained behind the mainstream society though there has been considerable relative improvement. Education, especially higher, has been recognized as a great equalizer and a powerful tool of upward social mobility capable of being used for reducing socio-economic disparities and building an inclusive society (Chauhan, 2011). However, Education ratio has become little high today in tribal women compared to past some decades but still it is not satisfactory due to some reasons mention earlier. There are many other reasons for low ratio of education in Tribal women i.e. women are not properly informed about the schemes introduced by Government, the funds provided for tribal women upliftment are not used properly, many women are not informed and aware of the welfare programs etc. Either Tribal women could not reach the welfare programs or welfare programs could not be reached the Tribal women soon. These are some clear and common causes for low ratio of education in Tribal women. As mentioned above, many schemes and policies are implementing to enrich education ratio in Scheduled Tribe women, though after seven decades of freedom they are still backward educationally. Here are suggesting some steps for increasing ratio of tribal women i.e. incentive scholarship should be given to the tribal female students, to provide them some basic amenities for education which deprive them from education, admission should be done on the base of reservation policy in educational institute along with some rectification, introduced awareness programs in educational institute to reduce the drop-out ratio, arrange the awareness programs for women at low income settlements and other settlements where large amount of population belonging to schedule tribes, stimulate the NGOs which are working for education of women in tribal areas, establish girl's schools and girl's colleges for socio-economically backward class, introduced professional courses in education institutes which indirectly motivate them for education etc. Through the help of education, tribal women would be able to realise about their rights, and it may be intervened to stop their exploitation at working place along with good wages of their hard work. In that context, we should make them realize the importance of education. As education is a weapon to win the world. Thus, these are some nominated suggestions which can uplift the ratio of women education in Scheduled Castes.

References

- Makwana M. H. (2000). *Gujarat ma Anusuchit Jaatio*. Vadodara, Surabhi Prakashan.
- Swami Vivekanada, (2005). *My India: The India Eternal*. Kolkata, Ramakrishna Mission Institute of Culture.
- Government of India (2001). National Policy for women empowerment, (excerpted from http://wcd.nic.in/empwomen.htm on 24 February, 2013).
- Chauhan C. P. S(2011). Participation of Women in Higher Education: The Indian Perspective, *Analytical Reports in International Education*, *4(1)*, 67-86.
- Census of India (2011). *State of literacy of Rural Urban Population*, Provisional Population totals, Government of India.
- Nayak, Debendra Kumar (2002). Gender, Caste and Discrimination: A Geographical Perspective on the pattern of literacy among Schedule Caste Women in Orisaa, *AJSDJ*, X, (excerpted from http://dspace.nehu.ac.in/ bitstream/1/3683/ 1/GENDER%20CASTE.pdf on 27 February, 2013).

- Makwana, M.H (2008). *Bharatiya Samaj Vyavasthaane Nari nu Sthan*. Vadodara, Surabhi Prakashan.
- Parmar, M. (2008). Dalit Nari Vikas-EkAvalokan, in M.H. Makwana (eds.), Surabhi Prakashan.
- Bhasin, Veena (2019). Status of Tribal women in India, (excerpted from www.ijims.com on 1st February, 2019).
- Chatterjee, Pujashree (2019). Social and Economic Status of Tribal Women in India- The Challenges and Road Ahead, (excerpted from www.ijims.com on 1st February, 2019).
- Short Essay on the meaning of education, (excerpted from https:// www.preservearticles.com/short-essays/short-essay-on-the meaning- of-education/17999 on 23-05-2019).
- Social and Health Status among Sahariya Tribal Women in Gwalior Division A Situational Analysis, (excerpted from https://www.researchgate. net/publication/ 336936951_social_and_heal'th_status_among_sahariya_ tribal_women_in_ gwalior_division_a_situational_analysis on 22nd march 2019).
- Wick Photos The Third Eye, (excerpted from https://phdphotos. blogspot. com/ 2011/04/womens-education-in-india-has-been one. html on 21st November' 2019).
- Dushi, Gauri (2013). Short essay on the meaning of education, (excerpted from http://www.preservearticles.com/2012010920245/short-essay-on-the meaning-of-education.html on 20 February, 2013).
- Muthumary, J. (2013). Dalit women in India, (excerpted from http://www. ambedkar.org/Worldwide_Dalits/dalit_women_in_India.htm on 25th February, 2013).
- Nira Desai (2012). 19 mi sadi ma samajikparivartan. Ahmedabad, University Granth Nirman Board.
- Rawal, Chandrika (2011). *Gender and Society*. Ahmedabad, Parshwa Publication.

7

Women Workers in Unorganized Sector: Reflections from Construction Industries from Six Construction Sites of North Kolkata

— *Dr. Sudeshna Saha*

Women are picking up sledge hammer, breaking down barriers and smashing gender stereotypes.........!!

The major part of the labour force in the developing nations is employed in the informal or the unorganized sector. Although it is difficult to give a concise and holistic definition of unorganized sector yet, unorganized sector covers about half of the GDP of our country. This preponderance of unorganized workers occupies almost 90 percent of the national labor force. This sector is characterized by seasonal employment (in agricultural sector), contractual work, no social security and welfare legislations, no rights and minimum wages. Lack of skill and education, few new openings in organized sector, unawareness of legal rights, deficient work quality and terms of service draws the labor into the available vortex of the unorganized sector. Here they face problems like poor health conditions, substandard working life, harassment at workplace, inadequate and unequal wage structures, long working hours, poor housing facilities, lack of safety measures, atrocities on women workers and no proper education for children of workers. Government intervention in taking necessary steps at the legal and policy level for unorganized workers is required for improving their working and living conditions (Rokade and Singh, 2015).

In the present paper, the researcher tries to make an attempt to understand the research related to the working and living conditions of workers in the unorganized sector and identify the gaps for further research.

For the same purpose, the researchers had interviewed female construction workers from six sites of north Kolkata and have collected some case studies.

Meaning of Unorganized Sector and Labour

The term "Unorganized" is defined as those workers who are not able to organize themselves to pursue their common interests due to certain constraints like casual nature of employment, ignorance, illiteracy, small and scattered size of establishment, etc. (Indushekara and Parashurama, 2014). An overview of the term 'unorganized sector' has been defined by the National Commission for Enterprises in the Unorganized Sector (NCEUS), Government of India as the sector which comprised of all unincorporated private enterprises owned by individuals or households engaged in the sale or production of goods and services operated on a proprietary or partnership basis and with less than ten total workers (Report on Conditions of Work and Promotion of Livelihoods in the Unorganized Sector, Academic Foundation, 1 Jan 2008, p.1774), (Dileep, 2013).

Easy entrance, local operations, ambiguous legal standing, ready requirement of labor, education and skill deficit, no fixed regulations of working hours or payment, poor rate of reparation, ignorance regarding and lack of possible government intervention and help characterizes this sector (Annette Barnaba et.al, 2009).

Characteristics of Unorganized Sector

Unorganized labor force stands for scattered and fragmented workforces working individually. They are not formally cohesive in any recognized association and union with defined ideology, goals and areas of specialization. India is one of the largest sectors in terms of employment of the unorganized sector of the economy workforce is concerned. It consists of agriculture and such related activities as forestry, livestock and fishing as well as nonagriculture (Manju, 2017).They do not have the collective bargaining power. Illiteracy, unscrupulous contractors and hazardous working conditions impose serious safety concerns for them. Longer working hours and job insecurity are other factors that such workers face. There is no social security for them except ESI. A majority of them live in slums or rented hutments with poor civic amenities. Employers and contractors to some extent, fulfill their economic and social needs (Das and Pandey, 2004).

This paints a dismal picture and the endeavor here would be to explore more about the working and living of these workers with a view to understand existing research and the gaps therein (Kapur and Sethy, 2014).

The unorganized labor is overwhelming in terms of its number range. As the unorganized sector suffers from cycles of excessive seasonality of employment, majority of the unorganized workers does not have stable durable avenues of employment. Their workplace is scattered and fragmented. There is no formal employer-employee relationship. In rural areas, the unorganized labor force is highly stratified on the basis of caste and community considerations. Workers in the unorganized sector are usually subject to indebtedness and bondage as their meager income cannot meet with their livelihood needs. The unorganized workers are subjected to exploitation significantly by the rest of the society. They receive poor working conditions especially wages much below that in the formal sector, even for closely comparable jobs. The unorganized workers do not receive sufficient attention from the trade unions. They have limited or no education or other skills, still today, they act as "bonded labor" in some cases due to low incomes & permanent indebtedness. High percentages of them are migrant labor (Rokade and Singh, 2015).

Women Workers in Unorganized Sector

The National Commission for Women estimates that 94 percent of the total female workforce is to be found in the unorganized sector. The presence of a vast multitude of women as workers and producers in the unorganized sector, where earnings are low, employment seasonal and insecure, supportive services woefully inadequate or even nonexistent, growth opportunities few and collective organization weak, has brought into sharp focus the failure of the mainstream to alleviate their predicament. While it is true that workers, irrespective of sex, are exploited in the unorganized sector, women suffer more by the fact of their gender. The changing patterns of economic development in the liberalization era have put a heavy burden on women, which is reflected on their health status. The small farmers, landlessness, forced migration both temporary and permanent, have undoubtedly affected women's health, nutritional and emotional status (Manju, 2017).

The growth of small and cottage industries has depended heavily on female labour. Women work in industries like tanning, tobacco, cashew, coir, textiles, garment, fish processing and canning, construction and domestic work, etc. In all these industries, they toil long hours at low paid, skilled or unskilled workers. As a result, they face serious health problems related to their work place, i.e. Occupational Health Hazards (Nadia and Mishra, 2017).

The risk of pollutants on women who work during adolescence, and pregnancy have serious consequences on women. Women work the most; paradoxically they earn the least in life. The additional social responsibility shouldered by them, their subordinate status in society, patriarchal family set up, socio-economic backwardness, proneness for occupation in the unorganized sector with low productivity and marginalization in employment opportunities account for their poor or low earning skills, illiteracy, ignorance and surplus labor and thus face high level of exploitation. This hampers their bargaining power for higher wages and any opportunities for further development (Manju, 2017 & Nadia and Mishra, 2017).

In the unorganized sector, work situations are not in official record and working conditions are not protected by law. So the problems of female workers in unorganized sector are not properly known. One of the major problems is that working conditions are worst. Due to population growth and urban migration, the active labour force was growing at a much faster rate than availability of jobs in the organized sector. The focus of development policies are gradually shifting from pure economic to growth with equity and the eradication of poverty (Manju, 2017), (https://archive.org/m/228workingconditionsandissuesofwomenworkersinanunorganized sector).

Construction Industries

Construction industry is the backbone of a country as it creates the infrastructure necessary for economic and industrial growth. In India, the construction industry is the second largest and a fast growing sector. Transnational companies have been competing in the construction industry since the mid-1990s, engaging in both large public-sector infrastructure projects and private sector industrial projects (Jhabvala and Kanbur, 2002). It employs large number of skilled, semi-skilled as well as unskilled workforce due to its huge demand in India (Rai and Sarkar, 2012).

In a globalizing economy, it is they who are constructing the new economy. India's three crore construction workers are literally the builders of modern India (Banu and Kumar, 2018).

They contribute in infrastructural development of India by building the roads and highways, the railway tracks and airports and ports, the IT cities, the call centres and mega malls that are creating new forms of wealth today. It is they who are laying the cables for a rapidly expanding country-wide telecommunications network that connect the vast sub-continent and make India one country, to shortening the distance and supporting the business activity in order to upgrade the economic development. Yet these workers, who are creating the base of the new economy, lives in a time warp, trapped in low skilled, low paid, insecure working conditions. The construction company is not making provision of any electricity or sanitation facility to these construction laborers. The sanitation hygiene of the construction site and the laborers' houses found poor condition. Majority sites do not have any toilets. Workers have to travel a distance to use the make shift toilets. Where the sites have toilets, it is having substandard quality. There is limited provision of drinking water and the laborers have to depend on bore well, tanker lorry water and public water supply. The construction company is not making provision of water facility for washing cloths and cleaning their utensils. The laborers have to depend on open well, public water supply, bore well, etc. Some of the construction companies are not making provision of facility for washing at all. Laborers have to depend on open bath, from where water available. This poses difficulties for women workers. Health of laborers is not at all matter to construction companies (Banu and Kumar, 2018).

Majority of companies do not pay medical cost incurred to the laborers. While a considerable number of site laborers and companies jointly meet the expenses incurred for the medical treatment. The women laborers are not eligible to get the maternity benefits. No holiday policy is found in majority construction sites. Moreover the companies are not ready to compensate with employees having partial and full injuries and are not covered by life insurance. Adequate accident relief equipments like helmets, hand gloves, shoes, safety belts, protective eye wear like safety materials and equipments are hardly provided to the construction laborers (Dileep, 2013).

The wage structure of the construction labor is also found inadequate considering their labor. Majority of laborers are getting wages in between 100-150 Rs/day. Here, the study observed differential wage system for the skilled and unskilled laborers. For the unskilled laborers the wage comes around Rs 150-200/day. The working hours of the construction laborers varied considerably. While majority of construction sites are making provision of 8-11 hour a day (Dileep, 2013).The laborers do not get healthy food from the construction site. Majority of companies are not making provision of better food to their laborers. Women laborers have to look after the food and home in addition to their regular work. The construction companies are not provided with crèches for the children. Majority of children are wandering around the site while parents working at the site. No one to look after these children and ensure their better health, education and care in their tender age. Many factors like frequent migration from one area to another; economic problems etc., cited by the construction laborers in making provision of better education for their children (Dileep, 2013).

Growth of Construction Sector Employment from 1999-2000 to 2011-2012 by major states

	Rural	*Urban*	*Total*
Andhra Pradesh	9.8	4.2	7.0
Assam	13.3	6.7	11.8
Bihar	17.0	10.3	15.8
Gujarat	4.1	1.1	2.6
Haryana	8.4	9.4	8.7
Himachal Pradesh	6.2	-0.3	5.9
J&K	11.3	6.3	10.1
Karnataka	9.4	3.0	5.3
Kerala	3.6	8.9	5.4
Madhya Pradesh	16.7	8.2	13.3
Maharashtra	8.2	3.1	5.2
Orissa	13.2	4.3	11.4
Punjab	10.7	4.2	8.9
Rajasthan	9.7	5.5	8.9
Tamil Nadu	12.2	3.9	8.8
Uttar Pradesh	14.2	7.5	12.6
West Bengal	14.1	3.8	9.9
All India	11.7	4.9	9.3

Source of data: NSSO employment and unemployment surveys (published reports and Velkoff and Adlakha, 1998)

Women in Construction Industries

Construction sector is the world's largest industrial employer with seven per cent of total world employment and 28 per cent of industrial employment. According to the International Labour Organization (ILO), construction jobs in most countries are undertaken almost exclusively by men. However, in the countries of South Asia, women often perform important but unskilled tasks for low pay. In India it is estimated that up to 30 per cent of construction workers are women. They are integrated into the bottom end of the industry, as unskilled workers or headload carriers (Patel and Pitroda, 2016).

But largely, this sector is male dominated. Of all the 10 million people employed in the industry, only 9% of construction workers are female. This figure is primarily women in administrative and office positions in construction, as the number of women actively working on construction sites is even smaller (https://theundercoverrecruiter.com/construction-needs-more-women). The construction sector has the largest number of unorganized labourers in India next only to the agricultural sector, and women form almost half the workforce as unskilled labourers with no occupational mobility. Often they face serious problems/ constraints related to work, viz., lack of continuity, insecurity, wage discrimination, gender and sexual harassment, unhealthy job relationship, lower wages, and poor job satisfaction. Despite these, construction industry overwhelmingly attracts female workers. Poverty being the main cause, the worst affected are the single and the derelict/ destitute women with children to support. Their husbands are often drunkards or are found to have other sexual partners and find themselves in debt trap. Unlike the womenfolk, men who come in as small boys, assist the masons for some years as helpers and finally, graduate as masons, some of whom later become contractors and move up the social ladder. Hence, the female labourers require empowerment through training and skill enhancement. The workforces employed in the construction industry have to face several hardships at the work since it is one of the hazardous occupations. Women workers are equally employed in this sector especially in unskilled category for sundry and manual works. They are working at various construction and project sites that are highly dangerous in nature and thus face several issues and challenges. Moreover about one-third of these workers in construction industries are women and children (Rai and Sarkar, 2012).

Women are almost unskilled labourers, they face serious problems related to work, viz., wage discrimination, gender and sexual harassment, unhealthy job relationship, lower wages, etc. despite all these, construction industry overwhelmingly attracts female workers (Rai and Sarkar, 2012). Their skills are always at the same level and are not upgraded as they assist only the male workforce at the workplace. The female employment in the construction industry is very high, even though they work only as the helpers or unskilled workers (Banu and Kumar, 2018). The present study aims at reviewing the existing literature to look for various issues of discrimination due to gender (Devi and Kiran 2013).

The construction industry is fret with problem like it is a maledominated field, females receive lower pay than male counterparts for the same level of work with no role models, discrimination, sexual harassment, limited training, unfair performance evaluation more clerical tasks, fewer leadership opportunities etc. Moreover, the nature of work leads to fatigue. Monotonous and repetitive work, work intensity, and duration of mental work, are some factors that require special attention. The workers even face anxiety when there is no work. The exposure to different environmental conditions like noise, light, and heat may be responsible for health impairment. Postural changes like bending forward or standing may cause backache, low back pain, neck pain and so on. It is also associated with weight bearing (Tiwari and Gangopadhyay, 2011).

Despite these problems, construction industry attracts female workers. Women workers perform various unskilled jobs at construction sites like cleaning building sites, earth work, carrying bricks, concrete blocks, aggregates, tiles, mortar, curing the concrete work and water up to the skilled masons, plumbers, tile, laying mason irrespective of the number of years they worked, they are not upgraded from unskilled to skilled as males. They are allowed to perform only certain types of work and usually they assist the male work force (Jhabvala & Kanbur, 2002; Baruah, 2010) in (Anvekar and Manjunatha, 2015).

Women are employed in semi-skilled and sometimes in skilled jobs in other industries but in the construction industry women are employed mostly as unskilled laborers (Jhabvala & Kanbur, 2002, p.7; Baruah, 2010) in (Anvekar and Manjunatha, 2015). Today Indian sub-continent is the second fastest-growing economy in the World. The Indian construction industry has been playing a vital role in overall economic development of the country, growing at over 20% Compound Annual Growth Rate over the past 5 years and contributing 8% to GDP. Due to mechanization in the construction Industry, liberalization of the Indian economy and the use of ready mixed concrete at construction sites, majorly women workers are employed to carry the raw materials for making concrete and placing the concrete manually. This also has resulted in the declining employability opportunities of the women workers (Anvekar and Manjunatha, 2015).

In today's scenario, it is important that women employed in the construction industries are treated and provided equal opportunities at par with the male workers to take up the other skilled jobs like mason, plumber, carpenter and painter etc so that issues like wage discrimination, gender bias can be eliminated which brings status of women workers in the construction trade in consonance with the other trades (Anvekar and Manjunatha, 2015).

This mindset has led to gender discrimination in this sector for work allocation and wage distribution (Suchitra and Rajshekhar, 2006). Such anti-women attitudes and discrimination has further complicated the workplace culture of these women labour. They live very tough life and do not enjoy equality of status and social justice for which they actually deserve (Anvekar and Manjunatha, 2015). It is evident that the overwhelming majority of women in the industry are young, being between the ages of 16-40 years. (Rai and Sarkar, 2012). Most of the women workers are married and young. Women of these age group have the capacity to do hard work and easily harassed by the contractor. Mason and labour contractors usually prefer to employ younger women whom they may exploit sexually (Anvekar and Manjunatha, 2015).

It has been observed that working conditions for women at construction project sites is not very good. Generally they will not be having separate toilets to use at job sites and most of the times have to share it with the male workers. Due to free mixing with the male co-workers, they might get Sexually Transmitted Diseases (Tiwari and Gangopadhyay, 2011). They are made to work more hours with lesser wages and there is no proper medical facilities and insurance for them, no medical, insurance, health, accident coverage .Usually the construction sites will not be having baby sitting or crèche if they having smaller children and their children have to spend time playing or sitting on the raw materials like sand or aggregates facing serious health issues (Anvekar and Manjunatha, 2015).

Very little is known about the role of women in construction industry and the factors hindering the equal presence of men and women, despite wide participation of women in science and engineering. The premise of WOMEN CORE is to determine whether women are under-represented in construction research and, how women's experiences may differ from those in the construction sector and those in academic and industrial research. Given the nature of both construction sector and scientific research cultures, it may be that construction research represents a 'double hurdle' for women seeking a career in this field (Patel and Pitroda, 2016), (Watts, 2007).

There are many studies discussing the reasons why female workers shy away from the construction industry as a whole and the craft sector in particular. Among the common barriers are social acceptances of employment, sexually inappropriate occupation, sexual discrimination, sexual harassment, physical incapability, unqualified for blue collar jobs and labour conditions such as extreme weather, unsociable work hours and exposure to hazards. Contrary, there have been few studies focusing on factors influencing women entry into construction and what their expectations are (Bennett et. al., 1999).

More specifically in the construction industry with the number of women presently low, the implication is that individuals, the industry, and ultimately the community all suffer the consequences of only fully utilizing the potential of one gender. Women are therefore, a wasted resource. However prevailing attitudes suggest change will not be easy because the dominantly male makeup of the construction industry is a deterrent to women who fear isolation, discrimination and harassment should they pursue careers in that sector. In most countries of the world the building industry is almost exclusively the domain of men (Patel and Pitroda, 2016).

In India, a large number of women are actively involved in the construction process itself. In spite of their large numbers, women construction workers are seen as secondary/temporary workers with seldom any opportunities for training, upward mobility, wage guarantee, fringe benefits or social protections. This study aim to explore role of women in construction industry and how it operates from the perspectives of the various role players in the industry, namely, the workers, contractors, intermediaries etc. The purpose is to map the existing knowledge base on the role of women workers and to identify from these mapping, key issues that need to be critically examined if opportunities for women in the industry are to be enhanced. The idea has been to make vivid the experience that women have on a construction site and draw from their account implications, issues and problems that one needs to address while formulating a public policy and modifying the practice. The construction industry remains one of the least researched industries in India. There is very little research published or reliable data on numbers, working and socio-economic conditions and the position of women workers within the construction industry (Patel and Pitroda, 2016).

Research Methodology

A combination of quantitative and qualitative research methodologies was used. Purposive sampling was used to carry out survey on 60 female construction workers. Data were collected on a one-to-one basis through semi-structured interview schedules and by non-participant observation in the 4 construction sites of north Kolkata. The researcher also considered six case studies of women workers at their same construction sites.

Field of the Study- Kolkata metropolitan city is the field area of study. The researcher restricted her study to 6 construction sites of Kolkata. They are Rajarhaat area, Baguihati, Ultadanga, Kakurgachi, Salt Lake and Tala Park areas.

Findings of the study

The researcher while during her study found out that the construction sectors are mainly dominated by the male workers. They are considered as more skilled, trained and more able bodied than the female construction workers. The latter is mostly considered as helpers in the sites. They are mainly used as cement and brick carriers to the actual construction floor. Whereas men are the real masons who actually build the buildings brick by brick. An attempt has been made in the paper to understand the socioeconomic condition of women laborers, nature of their work, their working conditions, wage pattern, wage discrimination, distribution and other difficulties faced by them at their work place. The researcher during her data collection from the field found that the women in the construction sites are basically migrant workforces who have migrated with or without their husbands in search of better work and pay.

Out of the 60 women interviewed from the six construction sectors, 80 percent of women are poor and lack economic capacity to feed their families. Mostly they are illiterate and have huge debts on their shoulders. The women workers in the Kakurgachi and Ultadanga construction sites, come by local trains from the fringes of the city and goes back by train as they could not afford to stay in the city. 30 percent among these women carry their little infants with them in the sites. These kids play and run in and around the construction sites much at risk and of accidents. Mostly they are unguarded and unprotected. Though Government have constructed schools for the children of labour forces, but most children remain away from it or they become drop-outs after some time. The women workers of the Rajarhaat and Baguiati stay in nearby slum dwellings. About 80 percent of the women workers interviewed under the study are poor female workers. Mostly mohammadens have migrated from Bangladesh. Post migration they are employed as daily wage earners in the construction of shopping complexes and apartment systems. While interviewing these women, about 34% among them, revealed that they face all sorts of emotional, psychological sexual harassment, gender biasness, wage discrimination and discrimination based on their minority status etc ., due to which the working environment becomes difficult for them in the industry and so they get demotivated to work and leave their job. 32 percent of these workers stated that they have a lot of mouths to feed. Their husbands are also not earning much. They are mostly into polygamous marriage staying with their multiple wives. They are mostly alcoholics and resort to domestic violence. These female workers in the Rajarhaat areas came to Kolkata for better future and pay. On interviewing the women workers in the Salt Lake construction sites, they briefed about their bitter working conditions. These women work on odd hours with no compensation. They even do not have proper toilet facilities in the site areas and often share it with their male counterparts. They are exposed to all abusive languages from their coworkers including their supervisors while at work. Issues related to health, job stress, and injuries at work place are the major concern for these women workers. Moreover these poor women feel unsafe while returning homes from work as Salt Lake area becomes a bit secluded at the late evening hours. Among them 27 percent women travel to Bidhannagar station and go to their respective homes in the vicinity of Kolkata. Some of them stay in the station areas. About 23 percent women narrated about their sorrowful status that they are compelled to indulge in other kinds of activities, including sex trade for extra money as they cannot feed all the mouths with their meager wages that they get out of their work in construction works. Women working at the Tala Flyover construction area, mainly stay as a makeshift arrangement near the construction sites itself. They are migrant laborers and do not enjoy any social security benefits. The socio economic challenges facing the women workers by dint of their work, their family liabilities and responsibilities of bearing, caring and rearing children make them to remain at a recipient's end as always.

Few Case Studies on Female Construction Workers in North Kolkata

Case Study 1- Falguni, from Rajarhat area, was 45 years old. She belonged to Bauri caste and had migrated from Murshidabad, West Bengal with her husband. After migration, she lost her husband to heart attack. She was left with no choice but to start working in the construction industry as a daily wage labourer at the construction site near Chinar Park. She earned Rs. 180 per day. One day she met with an accident while at work at the construction site. She fell down from the ladder with bricks loaded on her head. She sustained serious injuries on her head and back; and her whole body was bruised and wounded. She was hospitalized in an unconscious state. She went into coma and fought for life for nearly three weeks. At the work site, she was given some first aid only. She was removed from work after accident. She spent three months in the hospital and had to borrow approximately Rs. 40,000 from her relatives, neighbours and coworkers to meet the medical bills. After being discharged from the hospital, she continued to get frequent spells of unconsciousness, felt body pain, and weak for nearly six months. She was not taken back by the employer after her recovery. She did not receive any money as compensation. Therefore, she stared working as a domestic help to earn a living in nearby apartments.

Case Study 2- Mahnaz Pervez, is 34 years old. She migrated to Kolkata from Basirhaat with her children after her husband left her. After few months, she started working in a construction site at Baguihati area. Her day at work began at around 8am and ended at 5.30pm and later. She reported to have been exposed to lewd comments made by the people on the road as well as the coworkers. The work was very arduous and she was not happy with the wages she got. If she complained of anything, she was threatened to be fired. The construction site was not congenial for women to work. There was no proper space to sit, no canteens to have food. All of them used open space for urination. Water for drinking is also not clean. She cannot take her time off to look after her children; the children just roam here and there on roads, in sand or in mud. Most accidents take place in these construction sites as children loiter here and there and their mothers remain busy in construction works.

Case Study 3- Prabha migrated with her husband during the lean season of her village from Purnia district of Bihar. Due to financial instability and burden of three children, she joined the construction sector at Ultadanga, as daily wage earner along with her husband. She says that the work is not easy and they need to toil really hard under the heated Sun to get the minimum wages at the end of the day. They are not covered under any social security benefits, accident compensation, maternity leave, death claims. Their children do not get the educational benefits, medical needs. So Prabha is frustrated at the end of the day. Her husband being an alcoholic drinks every evening. So half of the family income goes away in alcoholism. If she obstructs then she is beaten badly. So she keeps numb and silently bear everything for the sake of her children. They have to stay in temporary unsettled accommodation and manage their household. They are often mistreated as they have no identity of their own.

Case Study 4- Sonali, a migrant labourer from Dhanbad, Jharkhand, started working in the Bagmari area of Kakurgachi, recollected the trauma of her husband who got paralysed during a fall from the construction site that rendered him to break his back and has difficulty in sitting and cannot walk. With little medical treatment, the condition has been worse now. The entire pressure of the family is at present on her. She has two daughters and one son. The daughters go to nearby school. There is hardly anybody to take care of them, as father is ill and mother is their sole bread earner. The Son is suffering from polio since birth. She too joined the construction industry after her husband's accident. But she laments that no medical help and accident benefit has been provided so far in compensation. She faces a lot of problem to take care of both her husband and son. She has to spend long hours in the construction site without any overtime. That takes a toll on her health. They are still not provided with any gloves, masks, safety shoes while working. So they have to bear several risks while at work. They also do not have any health insurance coverage. Constant financial crisis and loan from the contractors deter her from walking away from the construction sites and work elsewhere. They live in worse conditions with lots of debts on her shoulders.

Case Study 5- Najima Khatun, worked as a daily wage earner in construction site at Salt Lake, South Kolkata, recounts her frustration and daily stress in life after joining the construction sector. She says that she suffered from a miscarriage because of the daily pressure and workload. There is no facilities for maternity leave or no stipulated holidays for expectant mothers during and after their pregnancy. Though some companies unofficially provide maternity leaves. Furthermore these women face the worse form of humiliation from their supervisors and contractors if their work is not done properly and within the timeframe. There are no crèche facilities for babies of new mothers in construction sites. Even washrooms are common and in deplorable conditions. There is dart of clean and safe drinking water facilities within the construction sites. Moreover she also has to withstand the lewd and provocative comments from her fellow counterparts in the sites who get better pay than her because of the gender based wage division.

Case Study 6- Jyostna Bibi, a widow working in a construction site of Tala Bridge construction site area lamented sadly that, they are considered no one once the construction work is over. They are nameless entities, who neither possess any dignity nor identity. They are people just to get exploited day in and day out while at work in the construction industries. Back at home they live in deplorable conditions in jhupris (shanties) with daily struggle for their basic survival. The health of the construction workers hardly matters. She was stressing about her daily fight of life related to her health, her children's health, cooking hassles, using of community toilets, drinking water. Transfers from one construction site to the other. Daily hassle of heavy workload, less to meagre pay making these women's lives pathetic. So behind the glitz and glamour of city lights, there are gloomy stories of struggle, abuse, violence and violation of basic rights of life.

Summary of the findings

The study highlights the plight of the women construction workers. The fact of the matter lies that women have to struggle their way out. This industry lures helpless and naïve women workers for construction activities. They come for the sake of employment. But behind the facade of employability, they get exposed to various forms of atrocities and exploitation. The women are subjected to the worst kind of situation. Starting from low pay, to odd hours of job, lack of social securities, deplorable health conditions of women workers, domestic violence, poor housing and work conditions, alcoholic spouse, occupational hazards and lack of safety measures, poor wages, illiteracy of their children, sexual and other forms of exploitation at work etc rendered these women to be at the recipient's end. These sector is characterized by excessive seasonality of employment (especially in the farm sector), preponderance of casual and contractual employment, atypical production organizations and work relations, absence of social security measures and welfare legislations, negation of social standards and worker rights, denial of minimum wages and so on. Poor human capital base (in terms of education, skill and training) as well as lower mobilization status of the work force further add to the vulnerability and weaken the bargaining strength of these female workers in the informal sector. Thus, the sector has become a competitive and low cost device to absorb labor, which cannot be absorbed elsewhere, whereas any attempt to regulate and bring it into more effective legal and institutional framework is perceived to be impairing the labor absorbing capacity of the sector (Kapur and Sethy, 2014), (Rokade and Singh, 2015). Women need to raise their voices against all forms of atrocities and violent dominations. The civil society, Government and NGOs should also come forward for their rescue as and when it is required.

Conclusion

This research envisages adequate steps that to be taken by the policy makers and the building owners. Some of these steps based on the study is detailed as; Investigate the abuse and exploitation of laborers by agents and employees and prosecute such agents and employers. Create awareness of construction laborer's rights and set up mechanisms of redressal. Ensuring decent working conditions and proper contract systems and providing basic health care for construction laborers. Adequate intervention from the government authorities required ensuring the health, safety and welfare of the construction laborers.

Effective implementation of the labor laws that making provision of better health, safety and welfare of the construction laborers. NGOs working for child welfare should consider the difficulties of the construction laborers and plan strategies to ensure free education of these children. NGO's working should extend open education to the laborers and to alleviate atrocities against them. Organize public medical camps where construction sites are located. Constant inspection of the government part is required to reduce the plight of the construction laborers. Constructive support from the trade unions to the construction laborers to be ensured where the government and management couldn't support. Encourage the construction laborers saving habit by initiating thrift and banking awareness. Ensure adequate insurance facilities for the construction laborers. Ensure safety and security to the workers especially women workers in construction industry (Dileep, 2013). By safeguarding the rights and privileges of female workers, we shall pave the way for their empowerment. Once these women working in unorganized sectors get empowered, they shall be independent enough to take the right decision of their lives and their children. This move will incapacitate them to come out of the drudgery of day to day lives and move forward in their own space and live life in their own terms.

References

- Annette Barnaba et.al (2009). Study on the Empowerment of Women Construction Workers as Masons in Tamil Nadu, India. *Journal of International Women studies*, 11(2), 121-141.
- Anvekar, S.R. and Manjunatha, L.R (2015). *Women workers in* construction industry: issues and challenges relating working conditions in *Bengaluru*. Paper presented in National Seminar on Women in Informal Sector -Issues and Challenges, at Institute for social and Economic Change.
- Banu, R. & Kumar, S. (2018). Working Conditions and Issues of Women Workers in an Unorganized Sector-Special Reference to Construction Sector of Thuraiyur Taluk, Tiruchirappalli. *International Journal of Trend in Scientific Research and Development*, 2(3), 1369-1374.
- Barnabus et.al. (2009). A Study on the Empowerment of Women Construction Workers as Masons in Tamil Nadu, India. *Journal of International Women's Studies*, 11(2), 121-141.
- Baruah, B. (2010). Women and globalization: Challenges and opportunities facing construction workers in contemporary India. *Development in Practice*, 20(1), 31-44.
- Bennett, J.F, Davidson, M.J. and Gale, A.W. (1999). Women in construction: a comparative investigation into the expectations and experiences of female and male construction undergraduates and employees. *Women in Management Review*, 14(7), 273-291.

- Bino Paul G.D, Susanta Datta, Venkatesha Murthy R (2011). Working and living conditions of Mumbai Women Domestic Workers: Evidence from Mumbai Adecco from TISS Labor Market Research Initiatives (ATLMRI), Discussion Paper, 3-5, *Construction Management,* 347-356.
- D. Rajasekhar, Suchitra J.Y. (2006). *Employment Security for the* Unorganized Sector for the Unorganized Sector Workers in Karnataka, (Working Paper), Institute of Social and Economic Changes, 1-3.
- Das and Pandey (2004). Contract Workers in India: Emerging Economic and Social Issues. *Indian Journal of Industrial Relations*, 40(2), 242-265.
- Indushekara, G.V and Parashurama, K.G (2014). A Study on Rashtria Swasthya Bima Yojana for unorganized workers – with special reference to construction worker at Mysore city. *Acme Intellects* International Journal of Research in Management, Social Sciences & *Technology,* Conference On 'Indian Insurance Sector: Innovation, Sustainability and Social Impact' held on 22nd Nov 2014 Reforms through Research, 2 (1), ISSN 2320 – 2939 (Print).
- Jhabvala and Kanbur (2002). *Globalization And Economic Reform as seen from the Ground: SEWA's Experience In India,* (Working Paper), Department of Applied Economics and Management, USA, Cornell University.
- Kalpana Devi and Kiran (2013). Status of Female Workers in Construction Industry in India: *A Review. IOSR Journal of Humanities and Social Science* (IOSR-JHSS), 14(4), 27-30.
- Kapur, Surbhi and Prasana Sethy (2014). Working and Living Conditions of Workers in Unorganized Sector-A Review of Literature. *Online International Interdisciplinary Research Journal, 4(2)*, 197-204, (excerpted from https://www.researchgate.net/publication/260593434_Working_and_Living_Conditions_of_Workers_in_Unorganized_SectorA_Review_of_Literature on 12th December 2019).
- Kumar (2013). Gender Discrimination among Construction Workers with reference to Vijayawada. *Journal of Sociology and Social Work,* 1(1), 42-53.
- M. Dileep (2013). Inimitable Issues of Construction Workers: Case Study. *British Journal of Economics, Finance and Management Sciences*, 7(2).
- Manju (2017). Women in unorganized sector-Problems & issues in India. *International Journal of Applied Research*, 3(4), 829-832.
- Monisha and Rani,(2016). Women Working In Unorganized Sector-A Conceptual Study, *Indian Journal Of Applied Research,* 6(4), ISSN -2249-555X.
- Nadia A. and Pratibha J. Mishra (2017). Plight of women workers in unorganized sector of Bastar district of Chhattisgarh. *Journal of Social Work Education and Practice*, 2(1), 7-16.
- Patel and Pitroda (2016). The Role of Women in Construction Industry: An Indian Perspective, Proceedings from International Conference on Women in Science & Technology: Creating Sustainable Career (ICWSTCSC-2016), *Indian Journal of Technical Education* (IJTE) | Special Issue for ICWSTCSC-2016 ISSN: 0971-3034.
- Pini, B. (2002). Constraints to women's involvement in agricultural leadership, *Women in management review,* 17(6), 276 -284.

- Powell, A, Bagilhole, B. M. and Dainty, A.R.J. (2006). The problem of women's assimilation into UK engineering cultures: can critical mass work? *Equal Opportunity International,* 25(8), 688-99.
- Powell, A, Hassan, T, Dainty, A and Cartert, C (2007). *Strengthening women's participation in construction research in Europe*. In: Boyd, D (Ed) Procs 23rd Annual.
- Preet Rustagi, et al. (2003). Survey of Studies on Beedi Industry with Special Emphasis on Women and Child Labour, 9-16.
- Rai, A. and Sarkar, A. (2012). Workplace Culture and status of women construction labourers- A case study in Kolkata, West Bengal, *Indian Journal of Spatial Science*, 3(2) Winter Issue, 44-54.
- Rajasekhar D, et al. (2009). At times when limbs may fail: Social Security for Unorganized workers in Karnataka. *Karmayoga,* 1–32.
- Rokade, V and Singh, M. (2015). A Key Issues and Challenges of Working and Living Conditions of Unorganized Sector Work-Force in India. *New Man International Journal of Multidisciplinary Studies,* 2(6).
- Sandhya, et.al. (n.d.) *Women Civil Engineers in Construction Industry:* Issues and Career Challenges Relating Working Conditions in Bengaluru, paper presented at National Seminar on Women in Informal Sector -Issues and Challenges, At Institute for Social and Economic Change.
- Santosh Nandal (2004). Women Workers in Unorganized Sector: A study on construction industry in Haryana, *International Journal of Development* 5(2), 119-120.
- Santosh Nandal, (2006). Women workers in unorganized sector: A study on construction industry in Haryana. *International Journal of Development Issues,* 5(2), 119-132, https://doi.org/10.1108/eb045865.
- Suchitra J.Y. and D. Rajasekhar (2006). *Employment Security for The Unorganized Sector Workers in Karnataka,* (Working Paper), Institute for Social and Economic Change, 1-3.
- Tiwari, G., and Gangopadhay, P.K (2011). A Review of the Occupational Health and Social Security of unorganized workers in the construction industry. *Indian Journal of Occupational and Environment Medicine,* 5(1), 18–24, doi: 10.4103/0019-5278.83003.
- Vandana Dave (2012). Women workers in unorganized sector. *women's link,* 19(3).
- Velkoff, Victoria A and Arjun Adlakha (1998) *Women's Health in India*. U.S Department of Commerce, Economics and Statistics Administration, Bureau of Census. (Retrieved on 30.09.19) https://www.census.gov/ content/dam/Census/library/publications/1998/demo/wid98-3.pdf.
- Vijya Kumar Sodadas (2011). Unorganised Sector in India Working and Living Conditions of Stone Quarry Workers, 38-40.
- Watts, J.H. (2007). Porn, pride and pessimism: experiences of women working in professional construction roles. *Work, Employment and Society*. 21(2), 299-316.

- Watts, Jacqueline H. (2007). Porn, pride and pessimism: experiences of women working in professional construction roles. *Work, Employment and Society*, 21(2).
- Why the Construction Industry Needs More Women in Lead, (excerpted from https://theundercoverrecruiter.com/construction-needs-morewomen/ on 22-01-2020).

8

De-Gendering Women: A Human Rights Based Approach

— Dr. Swati Chakraborty

Introduction

During this decade, there has been a significant shift in approach to women's advancement and empowerment. While previously the advancement of women was regarded as important for outcomes such as economic development or population policies, more than ever the international community has come to consider the empowerment and autonomy of women and the improvement of their political, economic, social and health status as important ends in themselves (https://www.unfpa.org/resources/humanrights- women). This shift in approach reflects a human rights approach to issues of concern to women.

Parallel to this shift in approach to women's advancement has been an increased emphasis on the importance of a rights-based approach to planning and programming generally. In his reform proposals, the Secretary-General has made clear that human rights are a cross-cutting element that should be reflected in all United Nations policies and programmes. The High Commissioner for Human Rights is also stressing that human rights are integral to all activities, including peace-making, peace-keeping, peace-building, humanitarian assistance and development. Several United Nations entities, including UNICEF, UNFPA and UNDP have identified the securing of individuals' human rights as a critical first step in addressing global problems, and are now incorporating human rights into their policy making processes and operational activities.

Several factors explain these developments. First, the framework of international human rights law provides a forum for asserting individual claims of human rights violation. Some victims of human rights violation, including women who have suffered discrimination on the basis of sex, for example, those denied citizenship on the same basis as men, have successfully sought relief in international tribunals. The approach and decisions at international level have shaped decisions of regional and domestic tribunals, which have also provided remedies for individuals, including women, who have encountered denial of their human rights.

Perhaps more importantly, the language of human rights allows legitimate claims to be articulated with a moral authority which other approaches lack. It is a language which is recognized by the powerful, and which stimulates deep chords of response in many. It is a language which has the potential to empower individuals and communities at the grass-roots level to believe that they have a right to education, to health care or any other right. Human rights speak in broad terms about the fundamental entitlement of all human beings to live in dignity, and in conditions of social justice and thereby provide a foundation from which to establish a set of demands premised on the intrinsic worth of the individual. The human rights approach justifies legitimate claims, not because the realization of rights such as that to health or life is a means to another end, such as quality child care, environment, development or population policies, but because the realization of their rights is an important goal in itself (Raab, 1994).

Human rights also promise the engagement of the responsibility of the State in a way that other approaches to claims cannot. The conceptualization of a claim as a human right immediately involves the recognition of State and international responsibility if that claim is denied or violated. Concerns, when conceived of as rights, are elevated from the realm of State and international promises premised on good faith, to a level of legal entitlement requiring national and international response. Concerns, when conceived of as claims of human rights, become fundamental, immutable and priority claims.

Human rights not only create entitlements for rights-holders, but they also create duties for States. States are required to ensure the fulfilment of human rights by acting in a way that enables rightsholders to enjoy the rights to which they are entitled. Human rights require that actions - of a legislative, administrative, policy or program nature - are considered in light of the obligations inherent in human rights. Actions which violate or fail to support the realization of human rights contravene human rights obligations. A rights-based approach thus assumes the creation of an enabling environment in which human rights can be enjoyed. A rights-based approach also promises an environment which can prevent the many conflicts based on poverty, discrimination and exclusion.

Despite the recent focus on the rights-based approach, the meaning and practical implications of such an approach for policy making processes and operational activities, particularly in the context of development and humanitarian assistance, require greater clarity. This paper seeks to provide an understanding of the international human rights framework, and the challenges that must be addressed in integrating it into these processes in order to realize gender equality. A number of premises underlie the paper. First, human rights bring to the development discussion a unifying set of standards, or a common reference, for setting objectives and assessing the value of action. Second, that if sustainable economic development and the eradication of poverty are to be achieved, economic growth has to be combined with the concept of human development and respect for human rights. As such, the 'rightsbased' approach is an inherent dimension of the concept of 'people-centered sustainable development', with development constituting a comprehensive process directed towards the full realization of all human rights and fundamental freedoms. Third, central to the rights-based approach is the norm of gender equality, which resists, rather than accommodates, relativist approaches to the interpretation of human rights.

The paper begins with a survey of international human rights law, considering first, the development of international human rights standards and their reflection in regional human rights systems and at the domestic level. It moves on to consider gender-specific norms and standards, concentrating on the Convention on the Elimination of All Forms of Discrimination against Women. Critical issues relating to the scope and application of human rights are considered, including the identification of rights-holders and duty-holders and the nature of obligations of States as a result of human rights provisions. The role of civil society is discussed, as are challenges to a rightsbased approach to gender-equality, including the impact of the public/private divide and competing rights. The paper then examines the role of multilateral and bilateral entities in realizing human rights at the national level and concludes by proposing elements, which are inherent in a rights-based approach.

We can promote equality and women's rights by:

treating all staff and students fairly;

creating an inclusive culture for all staff and students;

ensuring equal access to opportunities to enable students to fully participate in the learning process;

enabling all staff and students to develop to their full potential;

equipping staff and students with the skills to challenge inequality and discrimination in their work/study environment;

making certain that any learning materials do not discriminate against any individuals or groups;

Ensuring policies, procedures and processes don't discriminate.

Women's Right and International Framework

Women play a vital role in poverty alleviation, which they are only able to do fully if they are empowered to by being granted basic rights. The advantages gained from realising a woman's rights to basic goods, education, political access and protection, etc. create positive ripple effects that help to ensure their children's education, reduce the rate of child mortality, increase the economic productivity of the communities in which they live, and more.

The inherent equality of the gender and the positive relationship between achieving actual equality and development is broadly accepted at the international level. The Convention on the Elimination of All Forms of Discrimination against Women (CEDAW), adopted by the General Assembly in 1979 and ratified by an overwhelming majority of states is often described as an 'international bill of rights for women and recognizes the fundamental "equal rights of men and women". Likewise, at the 2005 session of the UN Commission on the Status of Women (CSW), former UN Secretary-General Kofi Annan stated that "there is no tool for development more effective than the empowerment of women". Two of the Millennium Development Goals (MDGs), goal 3 – to promote gender equality – and goal 5 – to improve maternal health – are explicitly linked to women; and gender equality is mainstreamed into all the goals with the expectation that they are achieved in a non-gender discriminatory way.(Lee, 2005; May, 2001)

But whilst the role of women in development is recognized at an international level, the global failure to make a step-change in gender equality – typified by the woeful steps towards achieving MDG 5 – demonstrates a disconnect with actual progress. In this way, it demonstrates the fundamental difference, challenge and controversy of the rights-based approach to development. For it is not enough following a rights-based approach, to simply accept at an international level or in a donor country that the genders are equal and seek to 'improve the lot' of women; a true rights-based approach sees legal, social and attitudinal domestic change as a necessary condition of progress.

The recent developments in India represent a good example of how this change may look in practice. The Indian government ratified CEDAW in 1993, showing its international commitment to the rights of women. However, even before the 2012 gang rape and subsequent death of a 23-year of student in Delhi, the prevalence of discriminatory attitudes, institutionalized and exacerbated by a lack of access to justice, demonstrated a domestic disconnect with the principles underpinning CEDAW. While some practical and positive steps in empowering women had been taken in the country – through women's roles in microfinance, for example – their full capacity to both claim their rights and contribute towards combating poverty remained unfulfilled. The tragedy of the 2012 case and subsequent domestic outrage has provided pressure for legal change – such as the criminalization of marital rape – in the country, however, that may lead to the fuller realization of women's rights. In this way, the fundamental shift in attitudes (or at least a recalibration of the dominant socio-political view) towards women is driving forward progress.

Experiences such as India present a glimpse of the necessary steps that need to be taken for international development and help us to consider how those steps could be taken outside the context of a response to a national tragedy. The global experience of the disconnect between international commitments and the actual realisation of women's rights in-country must be considered if the post-2015 agenda is to more effectively achieve gender equality in order to drive development.

Women and SHGs

One of important questions can be asked i.e. Why Are Women Not Empowered?

They lack four basic things:

1. Knowledge
2. Finance
3. Power
4. Opportunity

Self-help groups fulfill the four criteria cited – thereby making them financially stable and also granting them a sense of empowerment.

Given the limited reach of government extension services in India as well as the potential gains from empowering women in agriculture, could another information delivery platform— women's self-help groups (SHGs)—be effective in providing agricultural information to women farmers, increasing adoption of improved agricultural practices, and increasing production diversity and market orientation? Local knowledge, social networks, and participatory training (neglected in traditional extension) are increasingly being recognized as important determinants of technology adoption and women's groups may be a promising platform to effect change on these fronts. (Bandiera et. al, 2018) Globally, women's groups have emerged as an important platform for promoting the economic, political and social empowerment of poor women, and in India, SHGs have become a central component of many rural development interventions (Ball, S. J., 1994).

Under the guidance of the National Rural Livelihoods Mission (NRLM) 3 and other NGOs involved in the formation and strengthening of these groups, SHGs in India are implementing interventions in agriculture and livelihoods. Professional Assistance for Development Action (PRADAN), one of India's largest NGOs, has worked with women farmers over the last thirty years both alongside and independent of the government, NRLM, and has pioneered efforts in providing agriculture extension for and through women's SHGs in rural India (Alkire, et. al. 2013).

Women's group-based livelihoods programs may improve agricultural outcomes through multiple pathways (Kumar et al. 2017). Multi-sectoral interventions such as PRADAN's typically comprise group formation and capacity building, savings and credit linkages, and livelihoods initiatives as independent but complementary inputs in improving women's role as farmers. These inputs can affect agricultural outcomes by (i) improving access to inputs, markets and technical knowledge, or the agriculture pathway, (ii) increasing access to finance, or the financial pathway and (iii) improving women's role in decision making on agriculture, or the empowerment pathway.

i. Agriculture pathway

Inputs provided by SHGs include dissemination of information on best practices through farmer field schools, demonstrations, promotional material, community trainers and exposure visits. SHGs supported by PRADAN are also involved in community sessions where they plan for agricultural seasons, and receive help in accessing input providers, government schemes, and markets. These livelihoods interventions increase women's exposure to better agricultural practices and crop selection, which in turn 5 leads to the adoption of improved agricultural practices. Assuming that there are no other constraints (for example, resource or access constraints) to the adoption of these practices, the possible outputs of this pathway are improved crop varieties, and an increase in yield or food production, market access and income from the sale of food or cash crops.

ii. Financial pathway

The financial pathway is the SHG savings and credit pathway. Typically, SHGs promoted by Government departments or NGOs are formally registered, conduct regular savings activities, open bank accounts, and access credit prior to undertaking income-generating activities. Participating in the SHG may increase members' ability to take loans, which is important for poor women who are not deemed creditworthy. Increased access to credit could increase household income and assets, and enable the household to smooth its consumption over time. Increased income could also relax budgetary constraints on the household's ability to adopt better agricultural practices, triggering the agricultural pathway.

iii. Cross-cutting pathway: Women's empowerment

Finally, the women's empowerment pathway underlies and interacts with the other impact pathways. This pathway operates through building social capital, taking collective action, and empowering women. We expect that the bundling of agriculture and livelihoods programs with the broader women's empowerment agenda will increase women's decision-making role in farming, which may improve her bargaining power, potentially improving health and nutrition outcomes.

Women and the Sustainable Development Goals (SDGs)

Gender equality is a right. Fulfilling this right is the best chance we have in meeting some of the most pressing challenges of our time—from economic crisis and lack of health care, to climate change, violence against women and escalating conflicts (https://eca.unwomen.org/es/news/in-focus/women-and-the sdgs).

Women are not only more affected by these problems, but also possess ideas and leadership to solve them. The gender discrimination still holding too many women back holds our world back too (https://eca.unwomen.org/es/news/in focus/ women-and-the-sdgs).

The 2030 Agenda for Sustainable Development and its 17 Sustainable Development Goals (SDGs) adopted by world leaders in 2015, embody a roadmap for progress that is sustainable and leaves no one behind (https://eca.unwomen.org/es/news/in-focus/women-and-the sdgs).

Achieving gender equality and women's empowerment is integral to each of the 17 goals. Only by ensuring the rights of women and girls across all the goals will we get to justice and inclusion, economies that work for all, and sustaining our shared environment now and for future generations (https://eca.unwomen.org/es/news/in-focus/women-and-thesdgs).

This editorial package showcases UN Women's 2018 flagship report, "Turning promises into action: Gender equality in the 2030 Agenda." It features data, stories, videos and publications that illustrate how and why gender equality matters across all the Sustainable Development Goals, and how the goals affect the real lives of women and girls everywhere (https://eca.unwomen.org/es/news/in-focus/women-and-thesdgs).

SDG 5: Achieve gender equality and empower all women and girls Targets (https://eca.unwomen.org/es/news/infocus/ women-and-the-sdgs):

- End all forms of discrimination against all women and girls everywhere.
- Eliminate all forms of violence against all women and girls in the public and private spheres, including trafficking and sexual and other types of exploitation.
- Eliminate all harmful practices, such as child, early and forced marriage and female genital mutilation.
- Recognize and value unpaid care and domestic work through the provision of public services, infrastructure and social protection policies and the promotion of shared responsibility within the household and the family as nationally appropriate.
- Ensure women's full and effective participation and equal opportunities for leadership at all levels of decision making in political, economic and public life.
- Ensure universal access to sexual and reproductive health and reproductive rights as agreed in accordance with the Programme of Action of the International Conference on Population and Development and the Beijing Platform for Action and the outcome documents of their review conferences.
- Undertake reforms to give women equal rights to economic resources, as well as access to ownership and control over land and other forms of property, financial services, inheritance and natural resources, in accordance with national laws.

- Enhance the use of enabling technology, in particular information and communications technology, to promote the empowerment of women.
- Adopt and strengthen sound policies and enforceable leg-islation for the promotion of gender equality and the em-powerment of all women and girls at all levels (https://eca.unwomen.org/es/news/in-focus/womenand- the-sdgs).

Women and girls, everywhere, must have equal rights and opportunity, and be able to live free of violence and discrimination. Women's equality and empowerment is one of the 17 Sustainable Development Goals, but also integral to all dimensions of inclusive and sustainable development. In short, all the SDGs depend on the achievement of Goal 5 (https://eca.unwomen.org/es/news/in-focus/women-and-thesdgs).

Gender equality by 2030 requires urgent action to eliminate many root causes of discrimination that still curtail women's rights in private and public spheres. For example, discriminatory laws need to change and legislation adopted to proactively advance equality. Yet 49 countries still lack laws protecting women from domestic violence, while 39 bar equal inheritance rights for daughters and sons. Eliminating gender-based violence is a priority, given that this is one of the most pervasive human rights violations in the world today. Based on data from 87 countries, 1 in 5 women and girls under the age of 50 will have experienced physical and/or sexual violence by an intimate partner within the last 12 months. Harmful practices, such as child marriage, steal the childhood of 15 million girls under age 18 every year (https://eca.unwomen.org/es/news/in focus/women-and-the-sdgs).

Women do 2.6 times more unpaid care and domestic work than men. While families, societies and economies depend on this work, for women, it leads lower earnings and less time to engage in non-work activities. In addition to equal distribution of economic resources, which is not only a right, but accelerates development in multiple areas, there needs to be a fair balance of responsibility for unpaid care work between men and women (https://eca.unwomen.org/es/news/in-focus/women-and-the-sdgs).

Sexual and reproductive rights are critical in their own right. Shortfalls in these multiply other forms of discrimination, depriving women of education and decent work, for example. Yet only 52 per cent of women married or in a union freely make their own decisions about sexual relations, contraceptive use and health care (https://eca.unwomen.org/es/news/in-focus/women-and-the-sdgs).

While more women have entered political positions in recent years, including through the use of special quotas, they still hold a mere 23.7 per cent of parliamentary seats, far short of parity. The situation is not much better in the private sector, where women globally occupy less than a third of senior and middle management positions (https://eca.unwomen.org/es/news/in-focus/women-and-thesdgs).

UN Women acts to empower women and girls across all its programmes and advocacy. With stepped up action on gender equality, every part of the world can make progress towards sustainable development by 2030, leaving no one behind (UNWOMEN) (https://eca.unwomen.org/es/news/in focus/women-and-the-sdgs).

While the world has achieved progress towards gender equality and women's empowerment under the Millennium Development Goals (including equal access to primary education between girls and boys), women and girls continue to suffer discrimination and violence in every part of the world (https://worldwomencongress.com/images/wcw-abstract-book-2019.pdf).

Gender equality is not only a fundamental human right, but a necessary foundation for a peaceful, prosperous and sustainable world. Unfortunately, at the current time, 1 in 5 women and girls between the ages of 15-49 have reported experiencing physical or sexual violence by an intimate partner within a 12-month period and 49 countries currently have no laws protecting women from domestic violence. Progress is occurring regarding harmful practices such as child marriage and FGM (Female Genital Mutilation), which has declined by 30 percent in the past decade, but there is still much work to be done to completely eliminate such practices (https://worldwomencongress.com/images/wcw-abstract-book-2019.pdf).

Providing women and girls with equal access to education, health care, decent work, and representation in political and economic decision-making processes will fuel sustainable economies and benefit societies and humanity at large. Implementing new legal frameworks regarding female equality in the workplace and the eradication of harmful practices targeted at women is crucial to ending the gender-based discrimination prevalent in many countries around the world (https://worldwomencongress.com/images/wcwabstract- book-2019.pdf). According to UNFPA statistics,

- Globally, 750 million women and girls were married before the age of 18 and at least 200 million women and girls in 30 countries have undergone FGM.

- The rates of girls between 15-19 who are subjected to FGM (female genital mutilation) in 30 countries where the practice is concentrated have dropped from 1 in 2 girls in 2000 to 1 in 3 girls by 2017.
- In 18 countries, husbands can legally prevent their wives from working; in 39 countries, daughters and sons do not have equal inheritance rights; and 49 countries lack laws protecting women from domestic violence.
- One in five women and girls, including 19 per cent of women and girls aged 15 to 49, have experienced physical and/or sexual violence by an intimate partner with the last 12 months. Yet, 49 countries have no laws that specifically protect women from such violence (https://www.unwomen.org/en/news/in-focus/women and- the-sdgs/sdg-5-gender-equality).
- While women have made important inroads into political office across the world, their representation in national parliament at 23.7 per cent is still far from parity.
- In 46 countries, women now hold more than 30 percent of seats in national parliament in at least one chamber.
- Only 52 per cent of women married or in a union freely make their own decisions about sexual relations, contraceptive use and health care (https://www.unwomen.org/en/news/in-focus/women and- the-sdgs/sdg-5-gender-equality).
- Globally, women are just 13 per cent of agricultural land holders.
- Women in Northern Africa hold less than one in five paid jobs in the non-agricultural sector. The proportion of women in paid employment outside the agriculture sector has increased from 35 per cent in 1990 to 41 per cent in 2015.
- More than 100 countries have taken action to track budget allocations for gender equality.
- In Southern Asia, a girl's risk of marrying in childhood has dropped by over 40% since 2000.

Conclusion and Remarks

Aptness towards the gender education in India along with other developing nations are still lacking behind even with lots of international and national rules and treaties. The concept of degendering has been emerged with the idea of women's rights from its own understanding with natural rights. Equality concept is underlying in this era of human development. Equality is ensuring individuals or groups of individuals are not treated differently or less favourable, on the basis of their specific protected characteristic, including areas of race, gender, disability, religion or belief, sexual orientation and age.

Promoting equality should remove discrimination in all of the aforementioned areas. Bullying, harassment or victimization is also considered as equality and diversity issues. While ostensibly communicating gender notions, local plans more normally reinforced conceptions of a universal humanity unintentionally concealing gender inequity. One can argue that although powerful interests operate a regulatory role through policy-making, funding, and appraisal (or sanction), local officials typically resist policy impositions either consciously (through forms of subversion), or unconsciously in willed or involuntary misinterpretations. The state may seek to enforce its desired outcomes through instruction and appraisal, but these modes bring about new tensions between different levels of the state. It would be misconceived, then, to understand the local state as either a passive recipient of policy or as simply a reproducer of dominant social relations. This level of the state, rather, exercises its resistance through rewriting, and failing to enact, policy, while complying with surface requirements.

References

- Alkire, Sabina, Ruth Meinzen-Dick, Amber Peterman, Agnes Quisumbing, Greg Seymour, and Ana Vaz. (2013). The Women's Empowerment in Agriculture Index. *World Development, 52*, 71–91. (excerpted from https:// doi.org/10.1016/ j.worlddev.2013.06.007 on 12-03-2019.)
- Ball, S. J. (1994). *Education Reform: a critical and post-structural approach*. Buckingham, Open University Press.
- Bandiera, Oriana, and Imran Rasul (2018). Social Networks and Technology Adoption in Northern Mozambique. *The Economic Journal, 116 (514)*, 869–902.
- Challenges and opportunities in achieving gender equality and the empowerment of rural women and girls, (excerpted from https://undocs. org/pdf?symbol=en/ E/CN.6/2018/3 on 12-03-2019).
- Hsiao, H. (1992). The rise of social movements and civil protests. Political Changing in Taiwan(eds.) T. J. Chen and S. Haggard, Boulder and London, Lynne Rienner Publishers.
- Kumar et. al. (2017). Pathways from women's group-based programs to nutrition change in South Asia: A conceptual framework and literature review. *Global Food Security, 17*, 172-185.
- Lee, S. C. (2005). *Women's movements and gender reform in education: comparative perspectives*, Paper presented in the Conference of Sino-Education, 25-27 Nov. 2005, Taipei: National Taiwan Normal University.

- Lee, S. C. and Hsieh, H. C.(2005). *The Formation of gender education policy: from education reform to Grade 1-9 Curriculum*, Paper presented in the Conference of Gender Studies and Public Policy, Taipei, The Graduate Institute of Gender Studies. Shih-Hsin University.
- May, T. (2001). *Social Research: Issues, Methods and Process* (3rd ed.). Buckingham, Open University Press.
- Raab, C. D. (1994). Where we are now: reflections on the sociology of education policy. Researching Education Policy: ethical and methodological issues (eds.). D. Halpin and B. Troyna, London and Washington, D.C, The Falmer Press.
- SDG 5: Achieve gender equality and empower all women and girls, (excerpted from https://www.unwomen.org/en/news/in-focus/women and- the-sdgs/sdg-5-gender-equality on 23-11-2019).
- Shelton, D. (2006). *Remedies in International Human Rights Law*. UK, OUP.
- Taylor, S., Rizvi, F., Lingard, B. and Henry, M. (1997). *Educational Policy and the Politics of Change*, London and New York, Routledge.
- The Human Rights of Women, (excerpted from https://www.unfpa.org/resources/human-rights-women on 12-08-2019).
- UNFPA (2006). The Human Rights of Women, (excerpted from https://www.unfpa.org/resources/human-rights-women on 12-02-2019).
- Women and the Sustainable Development Goals (SDGs), (excerpted from https://eca.unwomen.org/es/news/in-focus/women-and-the-sdgs on 12-04-2019).
- World Congress on Women-2019, (excerpted from https://worldwomencongress.com/images/wcw-abstract-book-2019.pdf on 12-04-2019).

9

Women in Sustainable livelihood: Case Study of Four Organizations across India

— *Dr. Neelmani Jaysawal*

Abstract

Sustainable livelihood is a terminology which equips an individual to cope and recover from stress and shocks for long term sustainability. It is a conglomeration of various elements which affect the livelihood for the future generation. In the words of DFID, Sustainable livelihood comprises of the capabilities, assets (including both material and social resources) for a means of living. A livelihood is sustainable when it can cope with and recover from stresses and shocks and maintain or enhance its capabilities and assets both now and in the future, while not undermining the natural resource base (Solesbury, 2003, p. 1). This concept which had first appeared in research literature in the 1980s, had become in the late 1990s one of a trio of principles underpinning UK development policy and the basis for a number of DFID programmes and practices (Solesbury, 2003, p. 1). In June' 1998, the Institute of Development Studies (IDS) outlined a framework for sustainable livelihood which had some interacting elements like context, resources, institutions, strategies and outcome (Solesbury, 2003, p. 9). In current period, the livelihood approach is being used very primarily by several civil society organizations. It seeks to improve rural development policy and practice through recognizing seasonal and cyclical complexity of livelihood strategies (Allison, 2003, p. 2). The livelihoods approach centres on the links between individual or household assets, the activities in which households can engage with a given asset profile, and the mediating processes (institutions, regulations etc.) that govern access to assets and to alternative activities (Allison, 2003, p. 4). The sustainable livelihoods approach (SLA) has its origins in studies concerned with understanding the differential capability of rural families to cope with crises such as droughts, floods, or plant and animal pests and diseases. Livelihood sustainability is also affected by external factors, sometimes referred to as the vulnerability context, comprising trends and shocks that are outside the control of the household. This paper intends to showcase the role of women in promoting sustainable livelihood based on some case studies.

Keywords: *Sustainable livelihood, vulnerability, assets, stress, shocks, social resource.*

Introduction

The concept of sustainable livelihood is very central to development discourse. The term 'sustainable livelihoods' relates to a wide set of issues which encompass much of the broader debate about the relationships between poverty and environment. This term was first introduced by the Brundtland Commission on Environment and Development, and the 1992 United Nations Conference on Environment and Development expanded the concept, advocating for the achievement of sustainable livelihoods as a broad goal for poverty eradication (Krantz, 2001, p. 1). It stated that sustainable livelihoods could serve as 'an integrating factor that allows policies to address development, sustainable resource management, and poverty eradication simultaneously (Krantz, 2001, p. 6). Yet in the existing literature, there is often little clarity about how contradictions are addressed and trade-offs are assessed. As Carswell et al (1997: 10) point out: "definitions of sustainable livelihoods are often unclear, inconsistent and relatively narrow. Without clarification, there is a risk of simply adding to a conceptual muddle (Scoones, 1998, p. 5)." Chambers and Conway define that a livelihood is sustainable when it can cope with and recover from stresses and shocks, maintain or enhance its capabilities and assets, while not undermining the natural resource base (Scoones, 1998, p. 5). According to him, the ability of a livelihood to be able to cope with and recover from stresses and shocks is central to the definition of sustainable livelihoods. Such resilience in the face of stresses and shocks is key to both livelihood adaptation and coping (Scoones, 1998, p. 6). The concept of sustainable livelihoods is a composite of many ideas and interests, the coming together of a number of different strands in the development debate. The important thing to recognise about the term is that it is always subject to negotiation (Scoones, 1998, p. 7). In order to create livelihoods, therefore, people must combine the 'capital' endowments that they have access to and control over (Scoones, 1998, p. 7). Within the sustainable livelihoods framework three broad clusters of livelihood strategies are identified. These are: agricultural intensification/ extensification, livelihood diversification and migration (Scoones, 1998, p. 9). The objective of sustainable livelihood is to increase the agency's effectivess in poverty reduction by seeking to mainstream a set of core principles and a holistic perspective in the programming of support activities to ensure that these correspond to issues or areas of direct relevance for improving poor people's livelihoods (Krantz, 2001, p. 18).

The Sustainable livelihood approach facilitates an understanding of the linkages between people's livelihood strategies, their asset status, and their way of using available natural resources, and is therefore a useful approach for understanding both the problem and the scope for promoting sustainable development at the local level (Krantz, 2001, p. 22). The sustainable livelihood approach shows the variety of activities to make a living. The Sustainable livelihood approach is one way of achieving poverty reduction, though there are also other strategies being pursued within the organization (e.g. macroeconomic growth, community development, community-based natural resource management, etc.) (Krantz, 2001, p. 12). It offers both a conceptual and a programming framework for poverty reduction in a sustainable manner. Conceptually, 'livelihood' denotes the means, activities, entitlements, and assets by which people make a living. Assets are defined as: natural/biological (land, water, common-property resources, flora, fauna), social (community, family, social networks), political (participation, empowerment – sometimes included in the 'social' category); human (education, labour, health, nutrition); physical (roads, clinics, markets, schools, bridges); and economic (jobs, savings, credit) (Krantz, 2001, p. 12). The sustainability of livelihoods becomes a function of how men and women use asset portfolios on both a short- and long-term basis. The Sustainable livelihood framework is built around five principal categories of livelihood assets, graphically depicted as a pentagon to underline their interconnections and the fact that livelihoods depend on a combination of assets of various kinds and not just from one category (Krantz, 2001, p. 19).

Sustainable livelihood- A gendered perspective

The livelihood may be sustainable not only due to its resistance to future stress and shocks but also due to women's attachment to it. The livelihood needs of men and women are not always the same because their roles, responsibilities, and resources are different. What is generally ignored is that the gendering of tasks is based on many other socio-cultural factors and socialization, rather than on natural or biological differences between women and men (Shangpliang, 2012, p. 480). Gender, the distinct roles, rights and responsibilities of men and women as determined by social and cultural norms and institutions (rather than biology) is increasingly recognised as an integral dimension of the institutional context affecting the achievement of livelihood outcomes (Stacey et al. 2019, p. 2).

Gendered division of work in all societies of the world is based on the naïve argument that women's tasks are less physically arduous than that of men; for this reason, when it comes to livelihood patterns, women tend to undertake roles that suit their physical strength, unlike men who undertake the more labour-intensive and managerial tasks (Shangpliang, 2012, p. 480). Gendered social norms, the informal and formal laws, beliefs and practices that help to determine collective understanding of what are acceptable attitudes and behaviours affect the opportunities available to men and women, with such norms often constraining women to traditional caring 'duties' within a household and/or work within the more vulnerable and undervalued informal sector (Stacey et al. 2019, p. 2).

Meanwhile, gender relations, the social relationships determined by expressions of power between men and women, directly impact access to, and control over, livelihood assets (including natural resources), as well as influence the nature and distribution of benefits of livelihood activities (Stacey et al. 2019, p. 2). Changing approaches to gender in development practice have occurred along two broad rationales. First, the inclusion of women in development was seen as having economic efficiencies (Stacey et al. 2019, p. 2). Approaches to gender can thus be conceptualised along a continuum from a 'gender reinforcing approach', to 'gender accommodating approaches', and finally a 'gender transformative approach'. Development programs applying a gender reinforcing approach may reinforce, sustain or take advantage of inequitable gender norms and power imbalances to achieve their objectives (Stacey et al. 2019, p. 2). Gender transformative approaches are based on a more complex and conceptually robust understanding of gender as a social construct, embedded in how societies define women's and men's roles and relations and the distribution of resources (Stacey et al. 2019, p. 3). The gender mainstreaming approach evidenced in the project where a gender action plan with participation targets guided and supported project activities and a gender consultant provided support for gender activity at implementation level. While documentation from several projects acknowledged the need for care in scheduling activities to maximize women's participation (i.e. balancing participation against a woman's need to care for children), only one project drew attention to the problem of seeking to increase women's participation in community-level governance process without first challenging local gender norms (Stacey et al. 2019, p. 10).

The inextricable link between land resources and rural livelihoods, along with increasing role of women as household providers in declining rural economies, stresses the need to consider the gendered terms of access and control of resource base, particularly in ecologically vulnerable regions (Shangpliang, 2012, p. 480). Most of women are actively involved in augmentation of forest resources and development of environment. It has come out in the preceding discussion that the women are the major gatherers of Non-Timber Forest Produce (NTFP) and that they are in the better knowledge of the important varieties of NTFP and the habitats where they thrive (Shangpliang, 2012, p. 486). The major reasons for women to engage in petty economic activities even though returns from such activities were not so much rewarding in monetary terms (Purbowo and Widodo, 2018, p. 347). The role of women tends to be subordinated by not being involved at all with either access or control on decision making of sugarcane farming. In addition, he argues that subordinate acts lead to an increase in feelings of disappointment, triggering an inferiority attitude and feeling concerned about his own circumstances (Purbowo and Widodo, 2018, p. 346). The increased role of women in the struggle for economic survival has not changed their position within the community rather it has tackled misery and destitution. The gendered perspective of sustainable livelihood states that there should be need to strengthen the space for women's independent reflection and expression: often bound by their socio-cultural and political environments, women, particularly those from the poor sections of society. The sustainable livelihood presupposes that through their active participation, disadvantaged people, of which women rank among the poorest, can determine and control the development process (Dem, 1993, p. 18). The strategy of gender-based livelihood is embedded into power relations whereby women tend to have less control over income and expenditures for household and family needs (Oberhauser, 2016, p. 491). Feminist analyses of livelihoods and natural resource use also focus on gendered aspects of the reliance of households and communities on natural products as sources of income (Oberhauser, 2016, p. 492). Gender relations are directly linked to colonial and other legacies of natural resource use and land distribution which have denied women equal access to land and resources (Oberhauser, 2016, p. 493). Feminist scholars argue that land redistribution should examine control over land as well as legal access to property. Overall, land reform that recognizes the role of gender and natural resources in convergent urban and rural spaces is crucial to balanced and sustainable development strategies (Oberhauser, 2016, p. 493).

Women are very much affected by economic crisis both in countryside as well as towns. Unemployment has increased the burden on women of making ends meet for the family. They are turning to the informal sector - a wide range of services and smallscale manufacturing - to keep the family going (Dem, 1993, p. 15). Another form of support has been in backing women's organisations so that they can act as a counter-balance to women's exclusion from the spheres of influence which affect their lives, and to their marginalisation, which is often linked to their lack of information and training (Dem, 1993, p. 16). To reduce rural households' vulnerability to food insecurity, women need to increase their sense of economic agency and physical capital empowerment to ensure stable off-farm incomes and giving households the capacity to survive shocks affecting food security (Sharaunga, 2015, p. 8). Women empowerment is also considered as a means to achieve other important livelihood outcomes such as more income (e.g., cash), increased wellbeing (e.g., non-material goods, like self-esteem, health status, access to services, sense of inclusion), reduced vulnerability (e.g., better resilience through increases in asset status), improved food security (e.g., increase in financial capital to buy food) and a more sustainable use of natural resources (e.g., appropriate property rights), improvements in child nutritional status and self-reliance (Sharaunga, 2015, p.1). The core outcome of women empowerment lies in the ability of a woman to control her own destiny and be self-reliant. Hence, selfreliance is an integral outcome of women empowerment, since; ideally, development should foster self-reliance (Sharaunga, 2015, p. 1). There has been a shift in focus on gender and agriculture to include new areas such as research on agricultural value chains and the impact of liberalization policies. Gender issues in community resource management have been researched by feminists mostly from the following two perspectives: a) gender impact of state programs on forest management, particularly on indigenous women or water resources management; b) women's movement against environmental degradation, for example, the literature on the Chipko movement (Nazneen, 2010, p. 12). Some of these are marked by gendered access, control, participation and/or have a gender differentiated impact (Nazneen, 2010, p. 13). This implies that analyzing how each institutional site is gender-biased and how this affects women's livelihood strategies provides a better entry point for understanding the gender dimensions of rural livelihoods (Nazneen, 2010, p. 13). The following parameters may showcase the role of women in sustainable livelihood through their involvement in multifaceted way.

Women and Agriculture

Agriculture is considered to be one of the occupations hugely dependent upon female workforce. According to World Bank et al. (2008), more women compared to men work in the agricultural sector, though their roles are unrecognized (Nazneen, 2010, p. 24). Many of the women may work as contributing family workers. The women are mostly involved into casual agricultural activity. In rigid forms of patriarchal systems, such as in South Asia, the absence of male support makes it difficult for women to access agricultural input and produce markets, information and government services (Nazneen, 2010, p. 24). A gender pay gap exists in these areas, and occupations are gender segregated, while the gender division of labor at home has not changed (Nazneen, 2010, p. 25). The average spending of time by women in agricultural activity is 7 hours each day which makes them core player in agricultural growth. The majority of women work as agricultural wage labor in addition to tending to their own fields. This factor combined with the time spent on household chores and child care (if any)—both of which are traditionally women's domain—leaves women with little time that can be set aside for group-related activities (Gupta et al. 2017, p. 1459). Female participation in agriculture is defined as the absolute number of females whose major economic activity is working in agriculture as either a cultivator or a laborer. Throughout India, women are more likely to be engaged in agricultural work than men, but, since much of this work is informally done as part of family's subsistence. The official statistics continue to grossly underestimate female workforce (Meena et al. 2018, p. 203). Women in eastern region of India have conventionally been involved in farm work in two main ways: as wage labourers (primarily during transplanting, harvesting, and in processing) and as housewives (in supporting roles and in market gardening) (Meena et al. 2018, p. 204). The study done by ICAR in Madhubani district of Bihar, it was found that among Women headed households (WHHs), about 25% owned the land they cultivated, followed by agricultural labourers (18%) and share cropper and owner cultivator (14%). Further, about 13% employed labour on their farms, while 12% worked purely as agricultural labour on other farms, and an equal number were pure share croppers (Meena et al. 2018, p. 204). As men move out of agriculture, women take up the roles of farm managers, farm labour as well as carers and primary providers of food security at the household level (Meena et al. 2018, p. 204).

Women and Water Management

Women are quite involved into water resource management. Women's relationship to water is considered to be non-monetary. Most of their time is spent in carrying water and ensuring availability of water for household chores. Gender intersects with other relations of power to "form and re-form our water world. In India, women are the single largest carriers of water into household. The role of women in water management plays a central role in safeguarding of water resources. It has become more common for women to be included in water use and water management institutions at a sub-national level, providing at least the possibility of gender issues being considered. However, at the international level, there is a general lack of incorporation of gender issues in transboundary water management institutions (Earle and Bazilli, 2013). The greater participation of stakeholders generally, and women specifically, in water management institutions is a relatively recent development, receiving official international recognition first at the UN Water Conference, in Mar del Plata, Argentina, in 1977 (Earle and Bazilli, 2013). As women are greatly engaged in the provision and management of water at the local level, this means they are directly impacted by the international legal agreements (Earle and Bazilli, 2013). It has become more common for women to be included in water use and water management institutions at a sub-national level, providing at least the possibility of gender issues being considered (Earle and Bazilli, 2013). k.10 In rural areas, poor households get their household water from community wells, nearby rivers or irrigation ditches, often involving arduous collection efforts (Bennett et al. 2008). Water is also an input for many traditional productive activities that women in Latin America carry out in their homes or on their land, both in rural and urban settings, including preparing food, baking bread, doing laundry for third parties, managing household vegetable gardens and raising animals (Bennett et al. 2008). Some women cope by hiring male helpers or relying on their male children to do the heavier work and attend water user meetings to speak for them. Some manage the whole process successfully against all the odd (Bennett et al. 2008). Sometimes women perpetuate their low self-esteem as they buy into the cultural code that water management is a matter for men and that women are only helpers. However, as soon as someone asks their opinion, women generally begin to speak out and dare to make decisions (Bennett et al. 2008).

Participation of women in water users' organizations for irrigation not only improves women's access to and control over irrigation but also may contribute to wider goals of women's empowerment (Bennett et al. 2008). Women were willing to take over the management of the village water supply. In fact twice they collected fund and repaired the system. Women looked upon canal water as if it was meant for domestic use and additionally for irrigation. The time spent by women in collecting water is known to have significant implications for their quality of life; the opportunity costs of time and energy spent collecting water have important implications for household food production and welfare (Narain, 2014). Gender equality and the participation of women and men are seen as ways of achieving more effective water policy and program outcomes and are considered key goals of integrated water resource management approaches (Narain, 2014). Development policy regarding women's role in water collection has often emphasized reducing time spent collecting water. Nevertheless, women's workloads related to water collection increased across all households, regardless of caste (Narain, 2014). Women in different life stages also experienced the impacts differently. Newly married women, for instance, perceived more intrinsic value in water-collection activities (Narain, 2014). Furthermore, the decline of common property water resource institutions (eg village ponds) may further increase dependence on water sources that increase women's workloads related to water collection (Narain, 2014).

Women and Natural Resource Management

Women are intrinsically connected to natural resources. Natural resource management is meant by management of resources like water, plants, forest, land through managerial aspect for its preservation for future generations. Natural resources are very vital for both rural and urban development. They are central themes for socio-economic development of any country. In this scenario, the role of women remains very crucial. The social relationships in which women are admitted, their status and the economic activities they are permitted to undertake, are strongly influenced by the rights to land. Both men and women are entitled to family land, yet women are given less to cultivate than men (Department of Planning and Coordination, Govt. of Nagaland, 2011, p. 4). Land is considered to be one of the productive natural resources where entire developmental activity is based.

Access of women to land, both arable and communal forest resources is critically important in India. It is a way to empower women. In most of India's rural context, women have only indirect rights to use the land via their husbands or a dominant male member of the household, and have no rights to inherit it however small in size it may be (Department of Planning and Coordination, Govt. of Nagaland, 2011, p. 4). Womens' lack of land rights can not only reduce the well-being of family but also deprive her socially and culturally. Hence, the effective exclusion of women from possession and control of land is largely the basis of their subordination and dependence on men in rural India (Department of Planning and Coordination, Govt. of Nagaland, 2011, p. 4). In natural resources, water is also considered to be a vital element. It is said that 4 billion people, that is half the world's population will live in countries with high water stress by year 2025 (Department of Planning and Coordination, Govt. of Nagaland, 2011, p. 19). More than 800 million people, that is, 15 percent of the world population, and predominantly women and children get less than 2000 calories a day due to poor water availability leading to poor productivity (Department of Planning and Coordination, Govt. of Nagaland, 2011, p. 19). The problems of water resource management or challenges are rarely connected to absolute resource constraints, but are closely linked to sociocultural, economic, political and institutional factors which govern the ways water resources are utilized and managed, to the extent to which groups in society are able to gain access to water resources for their specific needs (Department of Planning and Coordination, Govt. of Nagaland, 2011, p. 21). The availability of water resource, its management and distribution to the individuals, households, communities and among different user groups is critically important. Management of water resources is associated with household water supplies, irrigation, flood control, wetland preservation and fisheries (Department of Planning and Coordination, Govt. of Nagaland, 2011, p. 21). Women collect water and manage it for household use, ensuring adequate supply, storing and keeping it clean while stored in the house. They also play key community management roles in domestic water supply at community level including maintenance of traditional sources (Department of Planning and Coordination, Govt. of Nagaland, 2011, p. 21). In addition to water resources, forest resources are also vital components of natural resource management.

According to FAO (2005), 30 percent of the earth's land surface, which is a little below 4 billion hectares, is under forest cover. The world's forests are home to at least 80 percent of the terrestrial biodiversity that provide a major carbon sink to mitigate climate change (Department of Planning and Coordination, Govt. of Nagaland, 2011, p. 28). At global level, 60 million people are employed by forest industries. The forest plants provide pharmaceuticals and medicinal needs to about 1 billion people. It is evident that poverty in rural areas can be reduced only by sustainable management of our natural resources that generates both income as well as environmental services (Department of Planning and Coordination, Govt. of Nagaland, 2011, p. 28). The forests fulfill major economic functions, help maintain the fertility of agricultural land, protect water resources and reduce the risk of natural disasters such as landslides and flooding. Forests are therefore, the most important natural resources that provide immediate support to nearly half of the 2.8 billion people who live on less than a dollar per day (Department of Planning and Coordination, Govt. of Nagaland, 2011, p. 28). Community forest resources that provide environmental and ecological services are neutral to all living things including human beings (Department of Planning and Coordination, Govt. of Nagaland, 2011, p. 31). However, traditionally, community forest resource management, utilization, access to and control over the resources are gender specific and is predetermined by culture and tradition. For example, extraction, utilization and control of resources such as birds, animals, bamboo, cane, boulder and stones, trees for timber that can fetch monetary income fall strictly within the domain of males and hence, men are the primary users of productive forest resources (Department of Planning and Coordination, Govt. of Nagaland, 2011, p. 31). In this way, the participation of women in natural resource management has been very minimal.

Women and Employment

The role of women in sustainable livelihood may be witnessed in the area of formal and informal employment opportunities also. The feminization of the labor force is a global phenomenon. According to ILO(2008), about 200 million women joined the global labor force in the last decade. In 2007, there were about 1.2 billion women in paid work compared to 1.8 billion men (Nazneen, 2010, p. 27). Female labor is considered flexible labor for certain highly competitive, labor intensive sectors of global supply chains such as clothing, fresh produce, etc.

Female migration from rural to urban areas for work in manufacturing sectors has created opportunities for women to negotiate household relations. The women workforce is not only in formal employment sector but informal employment sector also. Women's informal employment comprises of 65 per cent of non-agricultural work in the Asia-Pacific (ILO 2002). Informal work includes workers in the unorganized or informal economy that include both employee and own account workers in nonagriculture and manufacturing employment (Nazneen, 2010, p. 39). The number of female workers in the informal sector has risen in absolute terms in South Asia, and compared to other regions, women's involvement in salaried work remains low (Nazneen, 2010, p. 28). The growth of home-based workers in South and Southeast Asia is a dominant trend in female employment. According to Doane (2007), women prefer homebased work as it allows for flexibility to do reproductive work. An income and social hierarchy exists among informal workers and the home-based workers are at the bottom of this hierarchy (Nazneen, 2010, p. 28). Informal workers have been incorporated into the global commodity chains to reduce costs. Different types of home-based work have developed, which reduce the cost of production by transferring part of the cost to the worker and economizing on the benefit accorded to formal economy workers (Nazneen, 2010, p. 39). Doane (2007) points out that gender is a key determinant of a worker's position within this hierarchy. Women may prefer home-based work as it provides flexibility for carrying out reproductive work. However, the nature of the work itself may be problematic as it isolates women from other women and public settings (Nazneen, 2010, p. 40). Kabeer's (2008) study on Bangladeshi women found that compared to women working in the informal sector or those not involved in the productive sector, women involved in paid work in the formal sector had more control over household expenditure, were most likely to buy assets, save and experience a higher level of mobility (Nazneen, 2010, p. 41). Studies conducted in India and Bangladesh show that there is a positive relationship between women's economic involvement and women resisting male control and trying to renegotiate gender power relations (Nazneen, 2010, p. 41). Generally, work outside the home leads to a shift in the domestic balance of power. Therefore, the employment opportunity and majority share of women in it has ensured increased participation of females in sustainable livelihood.

Women and Micro-Enterprises

The role of women in sustainable livelihood is very much explicit with its alignment with micro-enterprises. Micro-enterprises are small, labour intensive financed and managed by the owners which employ no more than ten workers (Nowak and Caulfield, 2008, p. 18). Women's inability to access formal institutions results into women's businesses frequently situated within informal sector. Women's businesses are more likely to be homebased and can be started quickly (Nowak and Caulfield, 2008, p. 18). The participation of women in micro-enterprises has positive results for women as well as their families and national economy. It has potential to help women in decision making process. Basically women entrepreneurs start their business with small scale and long scale business (Susruthan and Priyadarshany, 2018). Every woman entrepreneur strives hard to secure and serve the nation by making their business as a profitable. In the field of entrepreneurship, women entrepreneurs are also taking part and playing a vital role in this society. Women are highly empowered and motivated nowadays. So they also participate in all such activities to improve the economic status and economic growth of our country. Women entrepreneurs are trying to make a new environment and overcome all the hindrances which they face in this patriarchal society. Nowadays women entrepreneurs are also highly efficient in tackling the problems and use tactical solutions or way to run the business successfully. Women entrepreneurs run their business as of like men and women entrepreneurs are running business more efficiently than a men nowadays (Susruthan and Priyadarshany, 2018). Every woman entrepreneurs strives very hard to secure and serve the nation by making their business as a profitable and which should give a development to the country. Women entrepreneurs have increased the economic liberalisation and globalisation. These entrepreneurs have the role of change makers in both family and also in the society. Mainly women entrepreneurs give a larger employment opportunities towards women and also others this employment opportunities paves ways to the weaker section people mainly women and unemployed people in the society. They create a lot of awareness to the people by empowering women in both rural and urban areas of our society. In India, women enterprises estimated 10,63,721 of total in some states like Tamil Nadu, Pondicherry, Karnataka, Goa, Orissa, Lakshadweep, Kerala and Mizoram have women employment significantly higher when compared with other states (Susruthan and Priyadarshany, 2018).

In rural India, historically, plenty of girls number one producers can be categorized as entrepreneurs. For instance, a dairy farmer who resources milk to a close-by dairy or family is an entrepreneur. It is observed that women entrepreneur networks are major sources of knowledge about women's entrepreneurship and they are increasingly recognised as a valuable tool for its development and promotion. Policy makers must foster the networking of associations and encourage co-operation and partnerships among national and international networks and facilitate entrepreneurial endeavours by women in the economy. Increased participation of women in the labour force is a prerequisite for improving the position of women in society and self-employed women. Women's entrepreneurship deals with both the situation of women in society and the role of entrepreneurship in that same society. Women entrepreneur constitute 10 percent of the number of entrepreneurs in the country (Sharma, 2013). This has been a significant growth in self-employment of women with women now starting new ventures at three times the rate of men. They constitute 50 percent of the population of our country with a lower literacy rate than men (Sharma, 2013). Women-owned businesses are predominantly active in the consumer-oriented sector, that is more than 67 percent, compared to 45 percent of men-owned businesses, a sector generally characterized by ease of entry, but high competitiveness. However, women-owned companies promoting organic, conscious and local products in for instance the food and textile industries are increasingly gaining importance and make these businesses stand out, persist and what is more, make a difference (RiInvest Institute,

2017). In general, women are greater contributors to their communities' welfare either by reallocating their business profits or by acting as mentors to other women entrepreneurs. What is more, women are more direct contributors to their economies (RiInvest Institute, 2017). Women entrepreneurs seek out guidance from business support more often than men do, especially in the business initiation phase. Studies report that women who start and run businesses, mostly use informal sources of financing, such as their own or family savings, household income, equity from inheritance and credit from friends and family (RiInvest Institute, 2017).

Therefore, the role of women in promoting sustainable livelihood may be perceived through some selected case studies which are as follows:-

Case Study of Dharampur Utthan Bahini (DHRUVA)

The organization called "DHRUVA" has been involved in socioeconomic development of tribal community in Dharampur block in Navasari district of Gujarat. It has adopted a holistic view of development with natural resource base as core intervention area (IFAD, 2006). The organization selects one acre of plot where trees of mango and cashew are planted in each tribal area. All these activities are done with an active collaboration of women. It has also carried-out soil and water conservation like trench-cumbunds and micro watershed development programs (IFAD, 2006). Therefore, the organization in partnership with 19,000 tribal families is able to covert 17,000 odd acres of wasteland into productive orchards (IFAD, 2006). Since its beginning, 4,63,005 mangoes, 5,05,630 cashew and 79,22,300 forest trees have been planted (IFAD, 2006). More than 8000 wadi farmers have completed soil conservation activities in their plots.

Case Study of Lijjat-A Women's Enterprise

The enterprise called "Lijjat" is basically an attempt to attract the worldwide attention. Due to its adherence to core principles and practices, it lays its stress on management issues. This livelihood model can be emulated by people due to its sustainability framework. It helped the women to attain a sustainable income (IFAD, 2006). Beginning with 7 women in Mumbai, the organization has a total strength of nearly 42000 women across the country (IFAD, 2006). It is an excellent case of in-built expansion and diversification of a successful livelihood strategy. Recently, Lijjat has ventured into the supply of chapattis in Mumbai. It has engendered democratic principles through member participation as part of its administrative culture. The women members are decision makers in this organization. These women help each other to grow beyond the confines of their homes (IFAD, 2006). It is a symbol of women's strength. They take a greater responsibility and develop a sense of self-worth. The organization is based on this belief that the poor women are highly entrepreneurial and seek an enabling environment to realize their potential (IFAD, 2006). Lijjat has remained a member owned and managed body resisting the rise of a small managerial elite which takes control in such institutions (IFAD, 2006). There is a self-selection in terms of women with an entrepreneurial aptitude in the form of wages and shared profits (IFAD, 2006).

The organization is having notion of mutual trust, respect among its fellow women members. It has grown based on the strategy of backward and forward linkages. This organization is not a mere enterprise but a movement which has left a huge impact on women. This institution was created on the planks of collective ownership and management (IFAD, 2006). It is based on this belief that even poor women can take up responsibility of developing collective ownership and management. The Lijjat brand carried forward products much ahead of bigger competition. The marketing of Lijjat papad is supported by advertising division. According to Annual Report of 2003-04, the accumulated profits of Lijjat enterprise stand at Rs. 48.32 crores while the annual profit for the year are Rs. 6.54 crores (IFAD, 2006).

Case Study of The Co-operative Development Foundation in Andhra Pradesh

The organization called "The Cooperative Development Foundation" started its initiatives in Mulakanoor and its surrounding areas to tap the advantages of cooperative society. The organization was started in 1975 (IFAD, 2006). The efforts of association are highly innovative in their approach (IFAD, 2006). In its initial period, the staff of Cooperative Development Foundation (CDF) conducted a series of meetings to promote the Women Thrift Cooperatives. The approach of this organization was highly innovative in its approach and many successful banking and micro-credit initiatives emerged as a result of these efforts (IFAD, 2006). It works on the parameter that vibrant local economies may bring long term sustainable development to local communities and individuals. The dairy women cooperatives is managed wholly by women. The women members utilize the loans for productive purposes. The role of Cooperative Development Foundation was to motivate them to form cooperative societies and impart training on cooperative principle to its members (IFAD, 2006). One of the greatest roles performed by this cooperative society is to build confidence among women towards this society. It targeted poor women in its institution building measures. It has developed a truly democratic organization where poor women can participate (IFAD, 2006). A conscious strategy was adopted by this organization to bring social and economic benefits to the poor women. The initial approach of learning from the ground and taking lessons to wider forum are some of lessons adopted by this organization. This organization extended loans to their members for all economic and consumption activities.

Case Study of South Asia Poverty Alleviation Project in Andhra Pradesh

South Asia Poverty Alleviation Project is implemented in three districts of Andhra Pradesh to reduce the poverty. This project has facilitated organization of the poor into 2395 SHGs with 42842 members in 695 habitations in 20 mandals in these districts (IFAD, 2006). It seeks to alleviate poverty by involving the village community in the organization and management of developmental affairs (IFAD, 2006). With the support of various NGOs, SAPAP has been instrumental in institutionalization of three-tier people's organization like SHGs, VOs and Mandal Samakhyas. The efforts are made in the direction of formation of more SHGs and assist the groups to federate (IFAD, 2006). The core strategy of this organization is based on nurturing of people's institution and goal achievement. It has nurtured the Mahila Bank as part of its economic empowerment of women. The overall strategy of this organization is to build institution of women. Nearly 5200 SHGs of poor women has been promoted at grassroots level which has been further federated into 380 Village organizations (IFAD, 2006). The role of Mandal Mahila Samakhyas has been quite significant in the area of bringing collective bargaining power (IFAD, 2006). The NGOs have helped in the process of facilitating poor women to form groups. The organization impacted major aspects like micro-credit, social capital, poverty and women's empowerment through its intervention of SHGs and federations. All the SHGs have been federated into village-based organization by this organization.

Conclusion

The gender dimension of livelihood is quite diverse and complex. It indicates that established patterns of gender asymmetries regarding livelihoods are changing as more women enter agriculture labor markets and take up non-agriculture based work or diversify their livelihood strategies (Nazneen,

2010). In the area of livelihood generation, more women than men are involved. But there are some challenges which are crippling the growth of women. The increase in the number of women participating in agriculture and the diversification of livelihoods does not necessarily translate into being able to participate and take equal advantage of these opportunities compared with men (Nazneen, 2010). In South Asia, eight in ten women work in vulnerable forms of employment (Nazneen, 2010).

More women are vulnerable to economic shocks and crises compared to men. Women, as the trend for casualization and flexible labor increases, will find themselves without social security and protection (Nazneen, 2010). The growth of gender equality in rural livelihood is quite uneven. On one hand, it has increased women's well-being, on the other hand, it has not changed the gender division of labour. All of these indicate that there cannot be a blanket strategy/policy for attaining gender equality (Nazneen, 2010). It is also quite evident from recent studies that the poorest women are excluded from mainstream development. Building rural women's voice is a key area for promoting gender equality in various arenas related to rural livelihood. Building women's voice includes activities to open up formal policy spaces for actors who can give voice to rural women's livelihood needs (Nazneen, 2010). The centrality of gender equality, women's empowerment and the realization of women's rights in achieving sustainable development has been increasingly recognized in recent decades (UN Women, 2014). Gender equality can have a catalytic effect on achieving economic, social and environmental sustainability. Women have a vital role to play in achieving sustainable development. We recognize the leadership role of women, and we resolve to promote gender equality and women's empowerment and to ensure their full and effective participation in sustainable development policies, programmes and decision-making at all levels (UN Women, 2014). Women's knowledge, agency and collective action are central to finding, demonstrating and building more economically, socially and environmentally sustainable pathways to manage local landscapes (UN Women, 2014).

References

- Allison, E.H. (2003). *Potential Applications of a Sustainable* Livelihoods Approach to Management and Policy Development for *European Inshore Fisheries*, (excerpted from http://www.vliz.be/imisdocs/publications/74377. pdf on 22-07-2019).
- Baffoe, G. and H. Matsuda (2018). An empirical assessment of rural livelihood assets from gender perspective: evidence from Ghana. *Sustainability Science, 13*, 815-828.

- Bennett, V. et. al. (2008). Water and gender: the unexpected connection that really matters. *Journal of International Affairs, 61(2)*, 107-126.
- Bhattacharjee, M. (2010). Sustainable Livelihood in India: A Comparative Study between Rural and Urban Areas-A Case Study of Two Districts in Assam. *Asia-Pacific Journal of Rural Development, 20(1)*, 61-78.
- Dem, M. (1993). Sustainable Development: Women as Partners. *Focus on Gender, 1(1)*, 14-18.
- Department of Planning and Coordination, Govt. of Nagaland (2011). The Role of Women in Natural Resource Management-A Thematic Report, (excerpted from http://www.indiaenvironmentportal.org.in/ content/336833/the-role-of-women-in-natural-resource-management-a thematic- report/ on 25-07-2019).
- Earle, A. and Susan Bazilli (2013). A gendered critique of transboundary water management. *Feminist Review, 103*, 99-119.
- Gupta, S. et. al. (2017). Women's empowerment in Indian agriculture: does market orientation of farming systems matter?. *Food Security, 9*, 1447-1463.
- IFAD (2006). *Supporting Sustainable livelihoods-lessons from five case studies*, (excerpted https://www.microfinancegateway.org/sites/default/files/mfg-encase-study-supporting-sustainable-livelihoods-lessons-from-five-case-studies jan-2006.pdf on 24-06-2019).
- Krantz, L. (2001). *The Sustainable Livelihood Approach to Poverty Reduction-An Introduction*, Swedish International Development Cooperation Agency, (excerpted from https://www.sida.se/contentassets/ bd474c210163447c9a7963d 77c64148a/the-sustainable-livelihoodapproach- to-poverty-reduction_2656.pdf on 23-07-2019).
- May, C. et. al (no date). *The Sustainable Livelihoods Handbook-An asset based approach to poverty*, Oxfam, (excerpted from https://policypractice. oxfam. org.uk/publications/the-sustainable-livelihoods handbook- an-asset-based-approach-to-poverty-125989 on 18-06-2019).
- Meena, M.S. et. al. (2018). Participation and Perception Towards Changing Farming Practices in Eastern India: A Study of Women Headed Households. *National Academy Science Letters, 41(4)*, 203-205.
- Mehmeti, I. et. al. (2017). *Women's entrepreneurship-an analysis on doing business in Kosovo*. Kosovo, Riinvest Institute.
- Narain, V. (2014). Shifting the Focus From Women to Gender Relations: Assessing the Impacts of Water Supply Interventions in the Morni–Shiwalik Hills of Northwest India. *Mountain Research and Development, 34(3)*, 208-213.
- Nazneen, S. (2010). *Rural livelihoods and gender*. Asia-Pacific Human Development Report Background Papers Series, UNDP, (excerpted from https:/ /www.undp.org/content/dam/rbap/docs/Research%20&%20Publications/ human_development/RBAP-APHDR-TBP_2010_08.pdf on 18-04-2019).
- Nordic Consulting Group & Policy Research Institute (no date). *Women's Rights to Sustainable Livelihoods Project*, (excerpted from https://www. actionaid.org.uk/sites/default/files/publications/wrsl-flowexternal- evaluation.pdf on 18-04-2019).

- Nowak, B.S. and Tanya Caulfield (2008). *Women and livelihoods in Post-Tsunami India and Aceh*, Working Paper Series no. 104, Asia Research Institute, National University of Singapore.
- Oberhauser, A.M. (2016). (Re)constructing rural–urban spaces: gendered livelihoods, migration, and natural resources in South Africa. *GeoJournal*, *81*, 489-502.
- Purbowo and Widodo, S. (2018). A Study on the Impact of Commodity Changes to the Role and Strategy of Women's Livelihood. *Gender Issues*, *35*, 339-350.
- Rukmani, R. et. al. (2018). Women as Drivers of Change for Nutrition- Sensitive Agriculture: Case Study of a Novel Extension Approach in Wardha, India. *Agricultural Research*, (excerpted from https://doi.org/10.1007/ s40003-018-0383-x on 18-05-2019).
- Scoones, I. (1998). *Sustainable Rural Livelihoods: A Framework for Analysis*. IDS Working Paper 72, U.K, Institute of Development Studies.
- Shangpliang, R. M. (2012). Forest Legislations and Livelihood Strategies: Khasi Women in Rural Meghalaya. *Sociological Bulletin*, *61(3)*, 479-493.
- Sharma, Y. (2013). Women Entrepreneur In India. *IOSR Journal of Business and Management (IOSR-JBM)*, *15(3)*, 09-14.
- Solesbury, W. (2003). *Sustainable Livelihoods: A Case Study of the Evolution of DFID Policy*. Working Paper no. 217, U.K, Overseas Development Institute.
- Stacey, N. et. al. (2019). Enhancing coastal livelihoods in Indonesia: an evaluation of recent initiatives on gender, women and sustainable livelihoods in small-scale fisheries. *Maritime Studies*, (excerpted from https://doi. org/10.1007/ s40152-019-00142-5 on 18-04-2019.
- Susruthan, N.K. et. al. (2018). Role of Women Entrepreneurship. *International Journal of Pure and Applied Mathematics*, *120(5)*, 4199-4210.
- UN Women (2014). World Survey on the Role of Women in Development-Gender Equality and Sustainable Development. (excerpted from https:// www.unwomen.org/en/digitallibrary/ publications/2014/10/world-survey-2014 on 22-03-2019).

10

Impact of Digitalization on Women's Development

— Mr. Ashish Kumar Singh

Introduction

From a country of bullock-carts to becoming a hub for cyber-marts, access and affordability to information in India is now much easier. Every day there are billions of similar yet different activities taking place in the virtual world with the assumption that life has become easier, or, so to say, a click away; yet women maintain to live the secondary status in most parts of the world. The development approach has changed from looking at them as mere beneficiaries to active participants of the social change. Programs and resources are being directed to improve the situation of women. Digitalization has to an extent crossed the barriers of gender, class, caste and religion; however it alone cannot provide equal status to women. From election campaigns to sharing life-stories on social media, digitalization has taken us far away. The question of replacing human processes with digital ones has always been scrutinized. This chapter provides theoretical discussions as well as examples to describe the impact of digitalization on women's development using the available literature. Digitalization has changed our lives to a greater extent, that imagining ourselves without it can cause a serious socio-cultural trauma. Women in India, and in general, have been historically treated as second-class citizens with men not only making decisions, but also having access to all resources. This chapter presents the definitions of digitalization, and tries to show the relationship between women empowerment and digitalization.

Cases

First- a postgraduate student from America, Kate, visited Himalayan villages in Uttarakhand to learn about organic farming and migration. She took photos from her phone, recorded her conversations with the female farmers and made a video documentary describing the situation of those villages. Later Kate uploaded the stories of those rural female farmers of Uttarakhand on Vimeo to share it with her friends and colleagues.

Second- a Brazilian lady, Tania, in her 40s started teaching an online course on Community Healthcare for young mothers of her community in Bahia, Brazil. Combined with her own nursing experiences she brings in real life stories as case studies for her students. The program is gaining popularity, slowly, yet she is not disappointed, as she puts it aptly "it was getting tougher to find a suitable job. Internet helped me shape my life differently. I can spend a couple of hours every day working and spend rest of the time taking care of my brother and mother."

There are many sociological take-aways of these three stories. One of them is how the information and communication technology is giving access to information and connecting people across geographical and cultural borders. The examples above illustrate how technology and digitalization has an influence on each part of our daily lives, so much so that even during our interactions we tend to go back and forth towards technology to make the conversations livelier. Additionally, there is no difference in the way both of us are accessing the technology for communication and information sharing purposes.

When I started to think about this chapter, I had several ideas on how to structure it. Over time, I realized that in order to avoid too much complexity for each respective chapter I should begin by first presenting theoretical definitions and discussions for different keywords and phrases such as digitalization, digital divide. Further, this chapter will present discussions on gender digital gap and how to fill them.

Methodology and operational definitions

The chapter uses literature review as the method of inquiry, analyzing secondary data which has been accessed through platforms like Jstor, Informaworld and Google Scholar.

Digitalization is different from digitization and digital transformation. *DIGITALIZATION* is the process that restructures many domains of our social lives "around digital communication and media infrastructures, and how people interact, moving from analog technologies (telephone calls, snail mail) to digital ones (email, chat, social media), transforming the domains of both work and leisure". In other words, Digitalization can also be explained as the use of digital technologies to change a business model, that is, a process of moving to a digital business.

The Oxford English Dictionary (OED) defines *digitization* as "the action or process of digitizing; the conversion of analogue data (esp. in later use images, video, and text) into digital form", whereas *digitalization* refers to "the adoption or increase in use of digital or computer technology by an organization, industry, country, etc (Brennen and Kreiss, 2014)." Brennen and Kreiss (2014) provide the difference between digitization and digitalization. The former is the material process of converting individual analogue streams of information into digital bits; the latter, in contrast, is the way in which "many domains of *social* life are restructured around digital communication and media infrastructures" (Brennen and Kreiss, 2014).

Many scholars (Castells 2010, Van Dijkargues 2006 & Verhulst, 2002) point out that media and communications system have underlying value to explain many aspects of contemporary social life. Castells (2010) explains digitalization as one of the – if not *the* – defining characteristics of the contemporary era. Van Dijkargues (2006), "for the first time in history we will have a single communications infrastructure that links all activities in society". This new communication system known as 'new media' is transformed from the old media through the inclusion of digital technology.

German advisory council on global change defines digitalization as an unstoppable, accelerating process. Yet it is a development driven by humans, rather than 'force of nature'. Therefore, it inherits the capability of being be shaped. For it to be successful, the processes and effects of this technical revolution must be understood by the societal players, and its causes and drivers should be made transparent.Therefore, Digitalization is "the development and use of digital technologies and artificial intelligence to change a business model" and "provide new revenue and value-producing opportunities". It is the shift to a digital world, including e-governments, e-health, e-services, etc.

Women and Development

The Women and Development (WAD) approach began in the second half of the 1970s. The point of departure for WAD approach is the belief that women always have been part of development processes. Pala (1977, cited in Rathgeber, 1989) noted in the mid-1970s that the notion of "integrating women into development" was inextricably linked to the maintenance of economic dependency of Third World and especially African countries on the industrialized countries (Rathgeber, 1989). The WAD approach is broad in nature, as it focuses on the organic relationship between women and development, rather than just on policies and plans to integrate women into development. It starts with the point that women have always been integrated in the society. Their roles both inside and outside the house are important but such integration mainly sustains the inequality. Rathgeber (1989) writes that under this approach the under-representation of women in economic, political and social spheres is identified primarily as a problem that can be solved by carefully designed intervention strategies than by more fundamental shifts in the social relations of gender.

Digital divide and ICT (Information and Communi-cation Technology)

The "digital divide" is referred to as the gaps in access to information and communication technology (ICT) that threaten the ICT "have-nots". (OECD)

It can also be defined as the growing gap between the underprivileged members of society, especially *the poor, rural,* elderly, and handicapped portion of the population who do not have access to computers or the internet; and the wealthy, *middle-class, and young* people *living in urban and suburban areas who have access.* Education, income, race/ethnicity and gender area few main factors that influence digital divide.

Rogers (2001, 97) writes that there are similarities between digital divide and knowledge gap. As similar to mass media's infusion into social system with its expansion, population segments with higher socio-economic status tend to acquire the information at a faster rate than the lower status segments. Therefore the gap between different segments of society tends to increase rather than decrease. In Indian social system, women remain in the lower rungs of the society limiting their access and usage to technology, among other things. Access to information has the potential to change it from within.

Allwood (2017) writes that like any other phenomenon digitalization also has both good and bad sides. While today's discourse on digitalization consists of blockchain, artificial intelligence and crypto-currencies the questions related to the requirement of digitalization, replacing human practices, where and to what extent going digital are relevant. They shall be answered before any decision of changing course is taken. The important question one needs to answer here if the digital technologies are gender neutral, and if in any way they respond to the needs to men and women equally.

The World Economic Forum (WEF) report titled "Understanding the impact of digitalization on society" talks about how digital transformation can make positive contribution on society. The report indicates that digitalization may cause global job losses from 2 million to 2 billion by 2030. Uncertainty is also about its impact on wages and working conditions. Furthermore, the historic trend shows that for every 1% increase in global GDP, CO2 emissions have risen by approximately 0.5% and resource intensity by 0.4%, translating to $4.5 trillion of lost economic growth by 2030. Uncertainties in the job market and negative impacts of climate change affect women more, therefore, involving them in the digitalization processes, is crucial for current socio-economic growth of the society, as well as a need for equal future for all.

There are some questions that a digital and sustainable society needs to think through. These questions include the future of ecosystem and sustainable society, inclusive growth and poverty reduction, future of work and reducing inequality, broad-based work and required skillset, big data and privacy; and last but not the least about economic and political power shifts. These questions help to stimulate a debate on this topic and to encourage people to get involved in these developments with a holistic perspective in mind.

Studies predict that jobs that will become redundant including secretarial and office jobs, sales positions and low or unskilled jobs in the postal, courier services and storage sector, in the cleaning sector and in the restaurant and catering industry. There will job shift (i.e. the development of digital platforms and crowd-working, where workers from countries with high levels of social protection are competing with those from countries with low levels of protection and from developing countries) (Servoz, 2019). These changes will have an impact on the traditional understanding of employment, working time and place, and types of companies. It will give a chance to women to select their own work hours, giving them possibilities to shift between employment forms (part-time, full time etc.) more often. Workers will need to have more training and life-long learning. Digitalization also points to greater demands for specific type of jobs. A study by the World Economic Forum (WEF) states that although women are in some cases, such as computer coding are more competent on an overall basis than men, there is still a bias against them, to the point that women need to hide their gender when they submit their work. Studies show that the technology gap- in terms of access to internet- has widened from 200 million to 350 million between the years 2013-16. In Africa, women are 50 percent less likely to use the internet than men. Ownership and lack of control over the use of technology are other barriers affecting for women. In India and Egypt 12 percent did not access the internet more often because they did not think it was appropriate, and more than 8 percent did not access it more often because family and friends would not approve it. Moreover, more than 1.7 billion women globally do not own a mobile phone, whereas 80 percent of the developing world population has one. Cumulatively, these factors result in women not having the control to change their living conditions and environments, from economic opportunity to improving health outcomes, energy, environment and natural resource management and infrastructure development.

Huyer and Sukoska (2003) write that due to the capacity of ICTs to access, transfer and apply knowledge and information to almost every aspect of human engagement, they are being recognized as the careers of knowledge-based economy. ICTs carry multiple benefits for human societies; however these benefits are not evenly distributed between and among countries. Different factors such as gender, ethnicity, race and literacy level influence this disparity. Since ICTs are designed and created in male dominated environments, they do not necessarily correspond to the specific needs of women- resulting in a gender digital divide. Increasing level of education and globalization has changed the situation to some extent, by furthering efforts to have more inclusive ICTs will be a tool for women's empowerment.

Liff and Shephard (2004) write that there are arguments which state that every new technology has been adopted first by richer nations and wealthier citizens within them. Most technologies diffuse widely and the differences in ownership and use erode over time. Following this logic the diffusion of internet will happen automatically in time and hence does not need investment of public money to solve a problem that will solve itself. The parallel argument is that while the most obvious divide—the degree to which those using the internet are demographically unrepresentative—may be closing, other more subtle divides are emerging. These relate to the quality of access, ability to use the internet effectively and the way internet use affects access to goods and services (Liff and Shephard, 2004).

Access is an important factor defining and affecting digital divide from gender perspective. Access to internet (home as well work) were found to be significantly less available to women than men. Ability to use access differs for women and men. Liff and Shephard (2004) reiterate that women were more likely to think there were too much sex available on the internet and considerably more women than men mentioned their concerns about receiving unpleasant or spam e-mails. Gender differences were also found in respondents' accounts of how they learned to use the internet, with more women claiming to be getting help from someone. Men and women use technology differently, as a way to continue with their existing activities rather than as a stimulus for more fundamental changes in what they do. Similarly, a little gender difference was found in those who said that communicating with friends by e-mail was an important or very important motivation for initial internet use. The survey findings also suggest that while women are using the internet as an additional communication medium, it may be leading some men to maintain active relationships that they would not have done by other means. Men also reported checking their e-mails more frequently than women (Liff and Shephard, 2004).

Ching et. al. (2005) in a study conducted on American young adults write that having access to a computer at home at an early age. There are two possible interpretations of this finding, one is that some kind of critical developmental period exists wherein dispositions toward technology or technology skills facilitated via home access are formed at an early age and the other is that the home-age variable may reveal crucial information about what kinds of backgrounds these students are coming from. The issue of early socialization and values regarding technology leads into the question of how contextual importance and early school access faired in predicting full-spectrum frequency. It becomes obvious that the more important one considers a particular technology, the more one will use it.

Digitalization is also said to help people participating more in society, namely by facilitating access to information, creativity and empowerment. Social is understood as digital solution that may help people to access shared goods, facilitate sense of community without thinking much about scarcities of resources. However, digitalization also will widen divides in citizen participation, as the digital/tech savvy can participate the most, others cannot. These gaps can be seen in two different parts of a city, i.e. affluent or less affluent. Digital technologies need to work on delivering better care, and to enable people to live active and independently for a longer period. However, it requires a careful planning and inclusive approach.

Baglari (2014) writes that women from the grass root level are using ICTs to expand their mission, drive their passion to improve the world. Studies have suggested when women have access to educational resources, their families and communities benefit. Without computer access, the internet and technology training women will continue to be excluded from many opportunities for social economic leaderships. The World

Development Report (2012) by the World Bank and UNCTAD (2011) Information Economy Report demonstrate that providing women with ICT tools such as mobile phones can lead to a better quality of life and wider economic growth. Despite the fact that mobile phone are seemingly abundant, previous research shows that there is a significant gender gap in access to mobile technology in South Asia, where a man is 37 percent more likely to have access to mobile phone than a woman.

Swamy (2008) writes that the enabler approach to ICTs gives some gains from a gender perspective in that new technologies are seen as enabling women to better achieve various ends under the broad goal of bridging the digital divide. Through e-literacy and elearning programmes, women and girls can secure better education, similarly through information portals and centers women can get regular and required information on health, agriculture, livelihoods and job opportunities, through egovernance and computerization of public services, women can access their entitlements and get access to government programs and schemes. Unequal status of women impacts their access to social protection and their capacity to manage vulnerabilities, risks and crisis, including the domestic violence as some studies hypothesize that women's rights over ownership and control of property and inheritance would be protective for women from social and economic shocks (from those as well which arise from the experience of domestic violence). It is not clear to what extent ICTs can affect such structural issues, however process access to information, complain portals and a possibility to spread the stories world-wide through a click certainly helps.

The example of Radio Ujjas project by Kutch Mahila Vikas Sangathan (KMVS) in Gujarat, India and Deccan Development Society's community radio stations are worth mentioning in this context. In both of these places women-oriented radio programs have been established or where women-centered content is prioritized. Programs cover women's issues such as female infanticides, dowry, violence against women, collective management of resources and elected women representatives and other village-level issues.

(Swamy 2008) adds that in the information society, control becomes an important gender dimension, through women's ability to grasp, use and manipulate new technologies in ways that further their own cause Women's control over technology can strengthen their identity, inspire individual and collective action and bring about new and positive roles in the community. Women's movements now find ICTs as important part of their expansion. The recent example is the #MeToo movement, which has created huge uproar all across the globe.

Gurumurthy (2004) writes that the new ICTs provide opportunities to reorganize economic activities in ways that can bypass the traditional dependence of women producers on maledominated and exploitative marker structures, including middle-men. Initiatives such as 'Knitting Together Nations' (KTN) in Bonia-Herzegovania, Self Employed Women's Association (SEWA) in India and Les Pénélopes in France are some such examples.

We need to recognize the fact that old technologies are being successfully used in many places for spreading information about health, while the new technology is spreading. The Community Reproductive Health Project (REPROSALUD) in Peru, the usage of audio-visual medium by the Self Employed Women's Association (SEWA) to convey basic health information to women in India and Gindiku FM in Senegal are some such examples where the so-called old technologies are providing women a medium of their own (Gurumurthy, 2004).

Gurumurthy (2004) is right when he points out that the combination of New ICTs and old ICTs can offer many possibilities for non-formal and continued education, which have important gender implications. Azim Premji Foundation in India, Khan Academy and Coursera are some such platforms that are working towards bridging the digital education gap, by providing education content to the doorstep. Gurumurthy (2004) reiterates that the use of ICTs in governance has set the stage for greater transparency and the possibility for greater citizen participation. E-governance marks the shift towards greater access by citizens to public information and services, and to information about development programs and schemes particularly for the marginalized.

Bridging the digital gender gap

Sibthorpe et. al. (2018) writes that there are two main factors constraining women's participation in the information society: too many women face barriers to access and use digital technologies; and very few women are involved in the design, development, production and governance of digital technologies. The ITU (2017) estimates suggest that women globally are 12% less likely to use the internet. A recent GSMA study shows that in low- and middleincome countries, women are 26% less likely to use mobile internet than men, the primary means of accessing the internet in many parts of the world. The trend shows that women are more often under-represented at senior levels in high-technology industriesincluding the digital sector (https://www.gsma.com/latinamerica/wpcontent/ uploads/2018/07/ Policy_Brief_W20_DigitalInclusion_2018.pdf). The wide gender gap, in both developed and developing countries, starts at school level, continues into higher education choices and the workplace. The root causes of it are driven by a complex set of social, economic and cultural barriers, to overcome them targeted intervention by all stakeholders is required, which makes it difficult to predict whether this digital gender gap will close on its own (https://www.gsma.com/latinamerica/wpcontent/ uploads/2018/07/ Policy_Brief_W20_DigitalInclusion_2018.pdf).

The empowerment of women can take place through Employment, Entrepreneurship and E-governance by providing more flexibility, newer opportunities and easy access to information. Creating an environment to make women feel welcome and for comfortable learning, establishing ICT education center for women to provide them basic training in Internet use, MS-Excel, MSPowerPoint, computer basic etc, content in local language, more opportunities for women in leadership roles in ICTs companies, enabling women's participation in e-governance and building gender awareness among women and men participants, regular inputs from gender experts and organizations that work on gender issues and gender sensitization of people involved- are a few steps that India needs to take. Given that the society still unable to provide a basic minimum to a large chunk of the population, it becomes necessary to ensure the participation of women in each stage of digitalization. Examples and experience from many countries have shown that digitization can lead to empowerment of women; hence India should be hesitant in taking the necessary steps even if they seem risky in the beginning.

References

- Allwood, Jens. (2017). Is Digitalization Dehumanization?—Dystopic Traits of Digitalization. *Presented at the IS4SI 2017 Summit DIGITALISATION FOR A* SUSTAINABLE SOCIETY, Gothenburg, Sweden, 12–16 June 2017. *Proceedings 2017, 1, 259*; doi:10.3390/IS4SI-2017-04120.
- Baglari, J. (2014). Information and communication technology (ict) and women empowerment. *International Journal of Advanced Research in* Management and Social Sciences, 3(9).
- Brennen, S. and Daniel Kriess (2014). Digitalization and Digitization. Culture Digitally, (excerpted from http://culturedigitally.org/2014/09/ digitalization-and-digitization/ on 22-03-2019).
- Castells, M. (2010). Globalisation, Networking, Urbanisation: Reflections on the Spatial Dynamics of the Information Age. *Urban Studies, 47(13)*, 2737-2745.

- Ching, C.C, Basham J.D. and Jang, E. (2005). The legacy of the digital divide: Gender, Socioeconomic Status, and Early Exposure as Predictors of Full-Spectrum Technology Use Among Young Adults. *Urban Education, 40(4),* 394-411.
- Cooper, J. (2006). The digital divide: the special case of gender. *Journal of Computer Assisted Learning, 22,*320–334.
- Gurumurthy A, Singh, P., Kovacs, A. (2008). An Empowerment Approach to Gender Equality in the Information Society: Regional Analyses from Asia. *IT for Change.* (excerpted from https://itforchange.net/an-empowerment-approach-to-gender-equality information- society-regional-analyses-from-asia on 12-04-2019).
- Gurumurthy, A. (2004). Gender and ICTs-Overview Report. *Institute of Development Studies*, (excerpted from https://www.bridge.ids.ac.uk/reports/CEP-ICTs-OR.pdf on 12-03-2019).
- Huyer and Sukoska (2003). Outcoming the Gender Digital Divide: Understanding ICT and their potential use for the empowerment of women. *INSTRAW Research Paper Series Number 1. UNESCO, (*excerpted from http://www.onlinewomeninpolitics.org/beijing12/2003_gender_ict. pdf on 12-02-2020).
- Liff, S. and Shephard, A. (2004). An evolving gender digital divide? *Oxford Internet Institute, Internet (Issue Brief No. 2), (*excerpted from https://www.oii.ox.ac.uk/archive/downloads/publications/IB2all.pdf on 12-01-2020).
- Mazzarella, William. (2010). Beautiful balloon: The digital divide and the charisma of new media in India. *American Ethnologist, 37(4),* 783-804.
- Prasad, Kiran. (2012). *E-Governance Policy for Modernizing* Government through Digital Democracy in India. Journal of *Information Policy, 2,* 183-203.
- Recommendations for action: bridging the digital gender gap, (excerpted from https://www.gsma.com/latinamerica/wpcontent/ uploads/2018/07/Policy_Brief_W20_DigitalInclusion_2018.pd f on 12-05-2019).
- Rathgeber, E. (1989). Wid, wad, gad: trends in research and practice. *International Development Research Centre*, Ottawa, 1-26, (excerpted from https://idl-bnc-idrc.dspacedirect.org/bitstream/ handle/10625/5225/34345.pdf?sequence=1on 12-03-2019).
- Rogers, E.M. (2001). The Digital Divide. *Convergence*, *7(4),* 96-111.
- Servoz, Michel. (2019). The future of Work? Work of the future! European Union, (excerpted from https://skills4industry.eu/sites/default/ files/2019-05/AI%20-%20The%20Future%20of%20Work_Work%20 of%20the%20Future.pdf on 12-02-2019).
- Sibthorpe, C., Lopez, M. and Sticco, G (2018). Recommendations for action: bridging the digital gender gap, (excerpted from https://www. gsma.com/latinamerica/wp-content/uploads/2018/07/Policy_Brief_W20_Digital-Inclusion_2018.pdf on 23-01-2020).
- Suresh, L.B. (2011). Impact of Information and Communication Technologies on Women Empowerment in India. *Systemics,* Cybernetics and Informatics, 9(4).

- Swamy, GK, Ostbye T. and Skjaerven R. (2008). Association of preterm birth with long-term survival, reproduction, and next generation preterm birth. *JAMA, 299(12),* 1429-36.
- Teun A. van Dijk (2006). Discourse and manipulation. *Discourse and Society, 17(3),* 359-383.
- Verhulst, Frank C. (2002). Editorial. *The Journal of Child Psychology and Psychiatry*, 43(4), 415-416.

Index

V

W

Y